William Blake:
100 Selected Drawings

By Narim Bender

First Edition

Foreword

William Blake was English artist, draughtsman, engraver, philosopher, and poet, one of the most remarkable figures of the Romantic period. From childhood he possessed visionary powers, and the engraving of Joseph of Arimathea, done at the age of 16, shows him already using a personal symbolism to express his mystical philosophy. His apprenticeship (1772-79) to the engraver James Basire, for whom he made drawings of the monuments in Westminster Abbey and other London churches, led him to a dose study of Gothic art and intensified his love of linear design and formal pattern. In 1779 he entered the Royal Academy Schools, but his relations with Reynolds were painful; later he was to find more sympathetic spirits in Stothard, Flaxman, Fuseli, and Barry.

During the 1780s Blake worked as a commercial engraver, but from about 1787 he became engrossed in a new method of printing his own illustrated poems in colour, which he claimed to have been revealed to him in a vision by his recently deceased brother Robert. The first of these major works of 'illuminated printings'; in which handwritten text and illustration were engraved together to form a decorative unit, was Songs of Innocence (1789). In 1793 with his wife, Catherine Boutcher, he settled in Lambeth, where he engraved his principal prose work, The Marriage of Heaven and Hell. He had little material success and in 1800, at the suggestion of William Hayley, poet and man of letters, he left London to settle for three years at Felpham on the Sussex coast. Here he continued a series of watercolours illustrating biblical subjects for his first and most generous patron, Thomas Butts, and also began to engrave Jerusalem, the last and longest of his surviving mystical writings.

On his return to London, Blake made a series of drawings for Robert Blair's poem The Grave, and in 1809 held a small one-man exhibition for which he issued A Descriptive Catalogue, eloquently summarizing his aims and convictions about art. In 1818 he met John Linnell, whose sympathetic patronage ensured him a livelihood for the remainder of his life. For Linnell he carried out his engravings for The Book of Job and his magnificent designs for The Divine Comedy, on which he was working up to the time of his death. Linnell introduced to him a group of younger artists, including Varley, Calvert, and Samuel Palmer, who were inspired and stimulated by Blake's imaginative power. He thus passed his last years surrounded by a group of admiring disciples, who formed themselves into a kind of brotherhood called the Ancients.

In art as in life Blake was an individualist who made a principle of nonconformity. He had a prejudice against painting in oils on canvas and experimented with a variety of techniques in colour printing, illustration, and tempera. His work as an artist is almost impossible to divorce from the complex philosophy expressed also through his poetry. He believed that the visible world of the senses is an unreal envelope behind which the spiritual reality is concealed and set himself the impossible task of creating a visual symbolism for the expression of his spiritual visions. He refused the easy path of vagueness and misty suggestion, remaining content with nothing less than the maximum of clarity and precision.

To most of his contemporaries Blake seemed merely an eccentric, and his genius was not generally recognized until the second half of the 19th century. His output was enormous; there are important collections in the British Museum, the Tate Gallery, the Fitzwilliam Museum, Cambridge, and several American museums.

Drawings

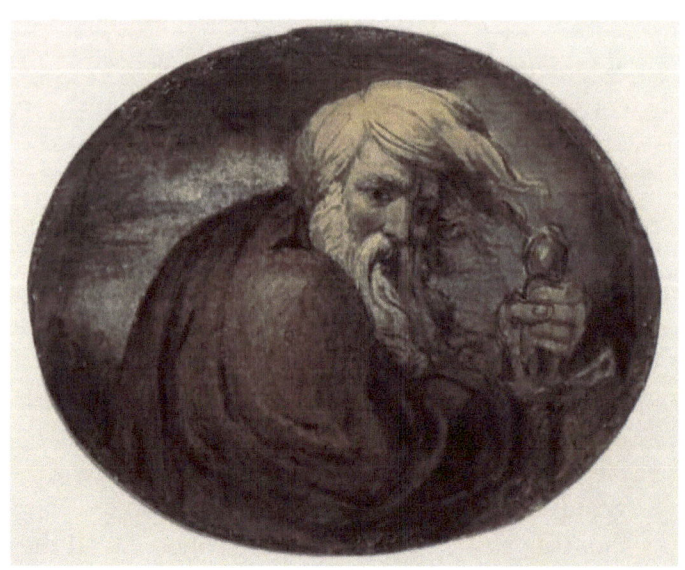

Lear Grasping a Sword

c.1780, Pen and watercolor on paper, 94 x 77 mm, Museum of Fine Arts, Boston

This is an illustration to Shakespeare's King Lear.

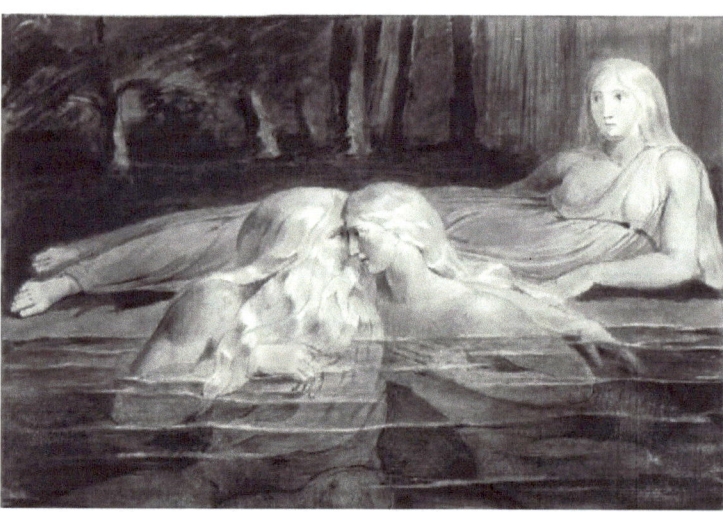

Har and Heva bathing: Mnetha looking on Tiriel

1789, point of the brush, Indian ink and grey wash on paper, 181 x 273 mm, Fitzwilliam Museum at the University of Cambridge

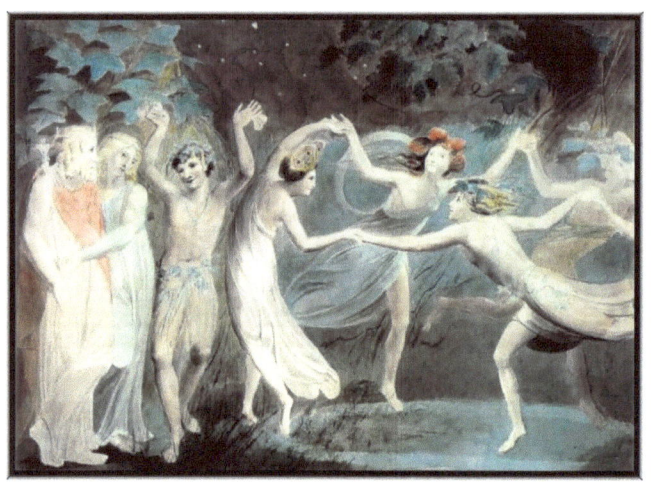

Oberon, Titania and Puck with Fairies Dancing

1786, illustration

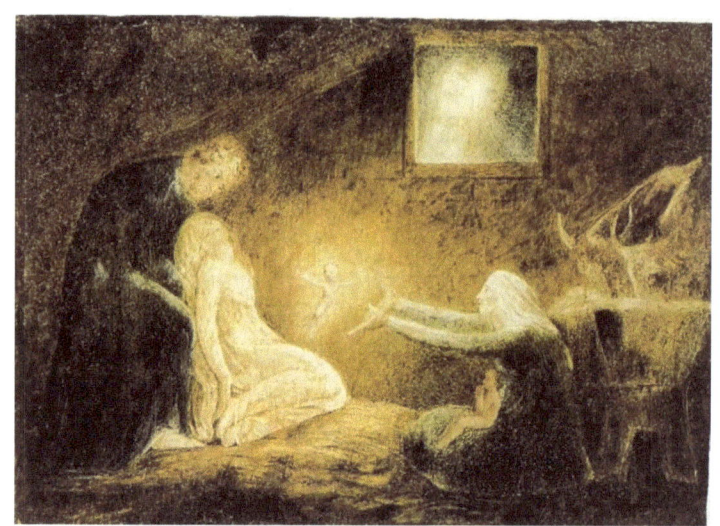

The Nativity

1790, tempera

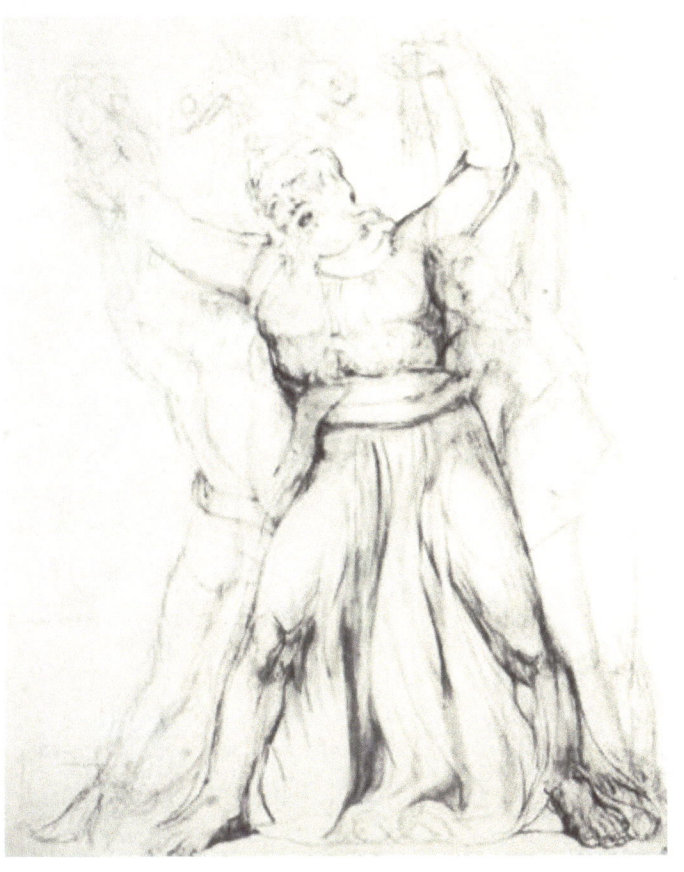

Laocoon

1790-1820, 38.1 × 25.7 cm, Pencil, pen and ink, tinted with ink on paper, British Museum

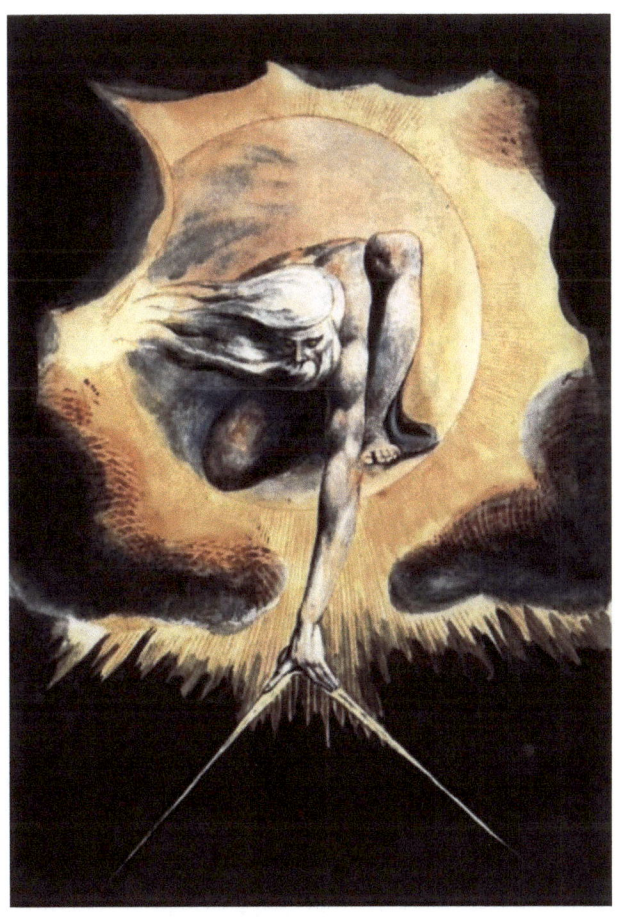

The Ancient of Days

1793, Etching, pen, ink, watercolour on paper, Stapleton Historical Collection, London

The subtitle of the picture is "Urizen measuring out the material world."

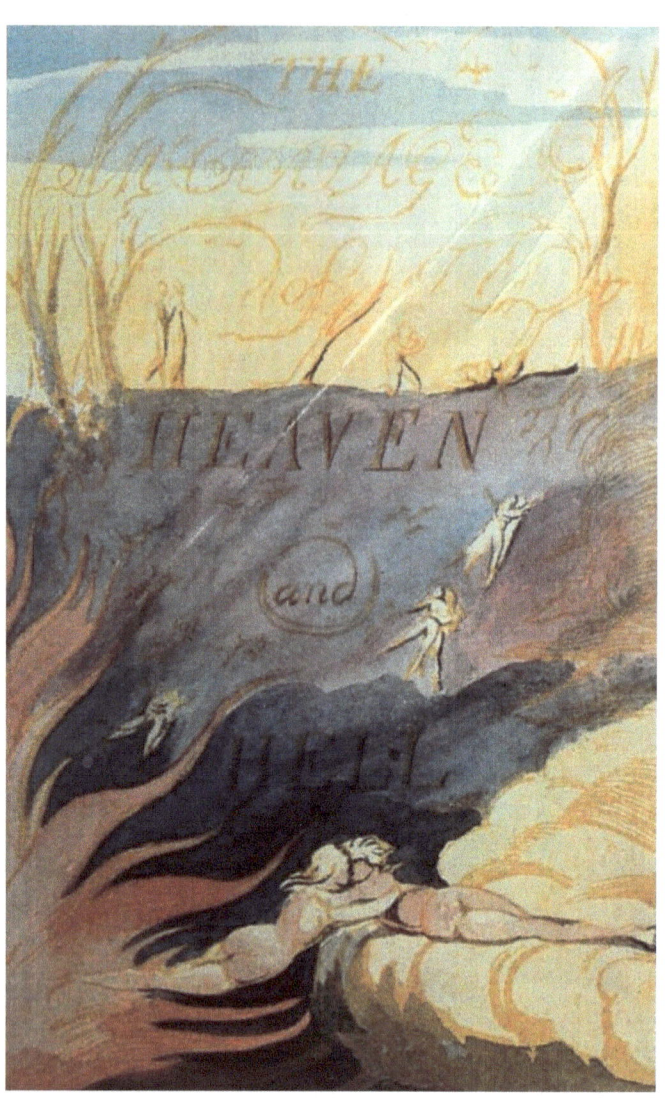

The marriage of Heaven & Hell, 1793

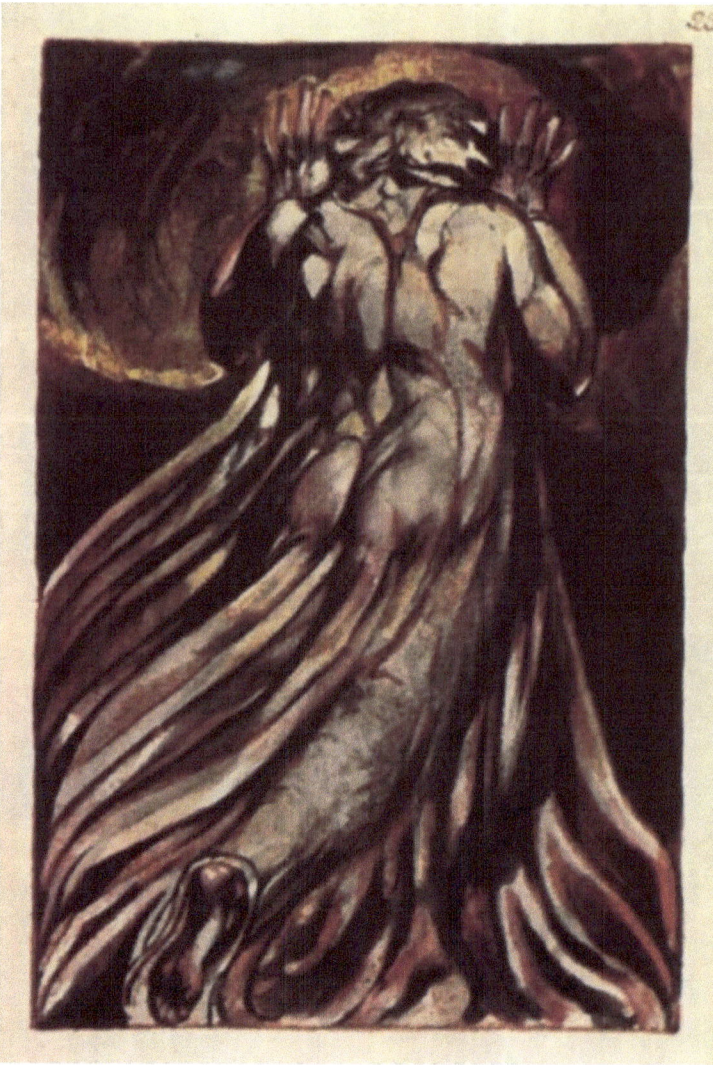

A white haired man in a long, pale robe who
flees from us with his hands raised, 1794

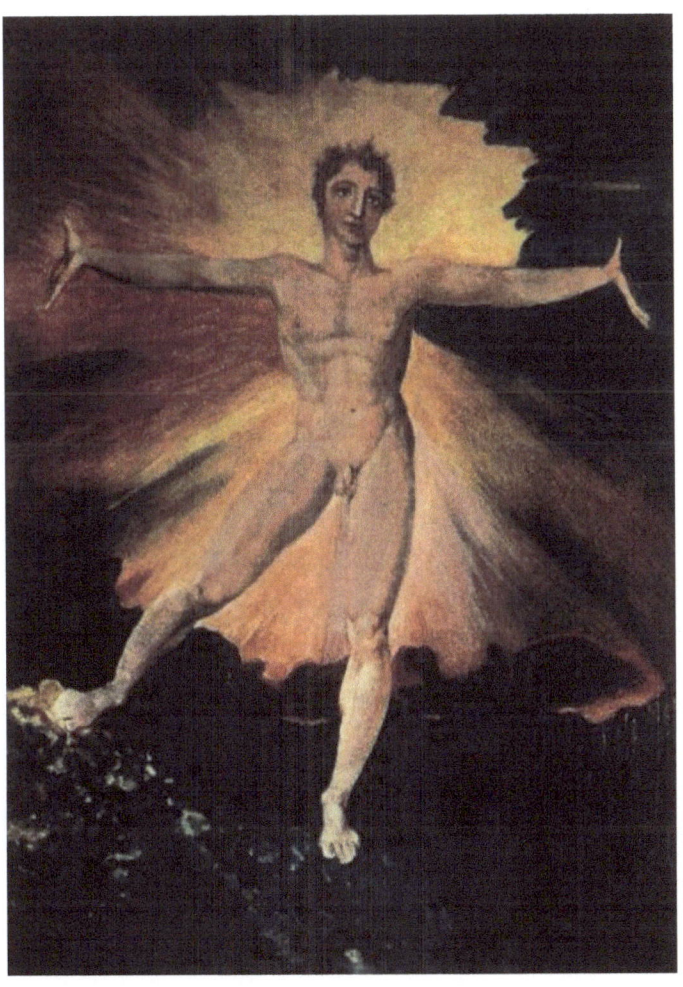

Glad Day or The Dance of Albion, 1794

Blake produced in the mid-1790s a series of large colour prints on themes of oppression, one of which is Nebuchadnezzar. This plate depicts the animal state to which man had been reduced after the Fall, so vividly personified in the crouching form and sullen stare of his Nebuchadnezzar.

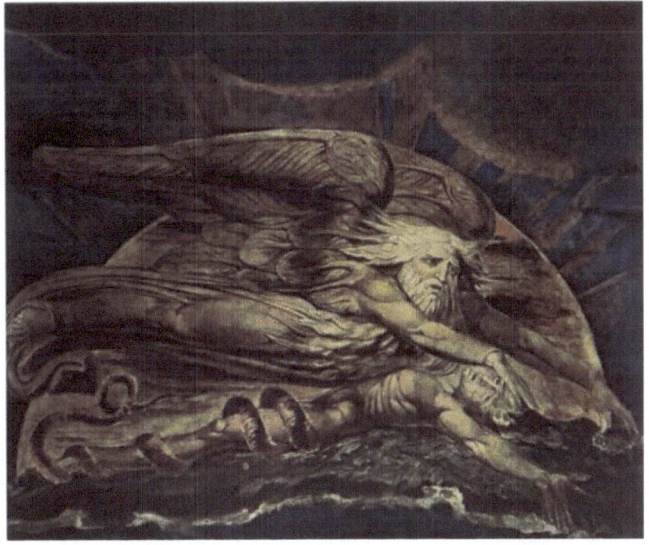

And Elohim created Adam, 1795

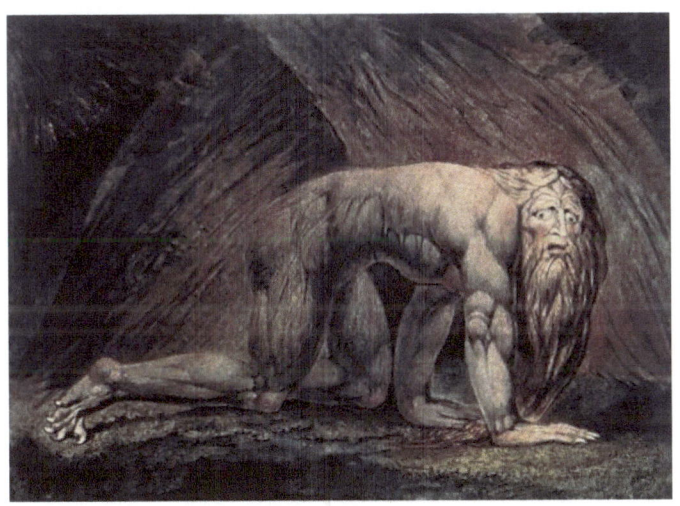

Nebuchadnezzar

1795, Copper engraving with pen and ink and watercolour, 446 x 620 mm, Tate Gallery, London

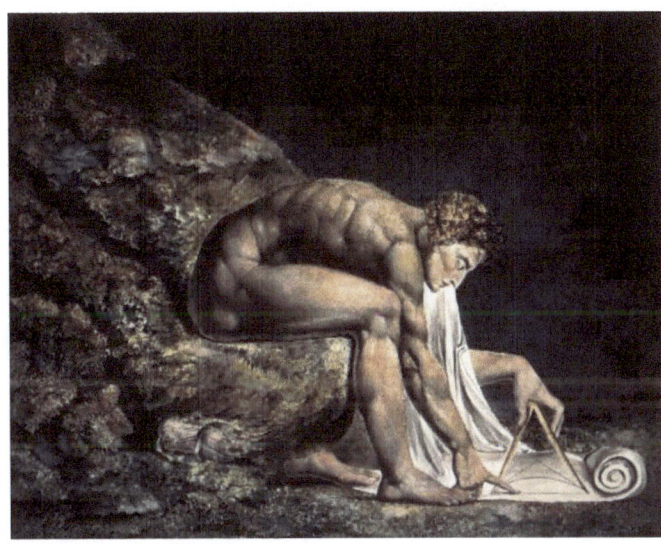

Isaac Newton

1795, Copper engraving with pen and ink and watercolour, 460 x 600 mm, Tate Gallery, London

Blake sought to exemplify the deeper significance of his philosophical thought in the tension between the immediate realism of his image and fantastic symbolism.

Newton, man naked and created out of chaos, appears to be breaking through the chaos. He is discovering the law that is inherent in his own physical nature. Man has tasted of the fruit of the tree of knowledge, and now his intellect reveals to his astonished gaze the abstract reality of creation.

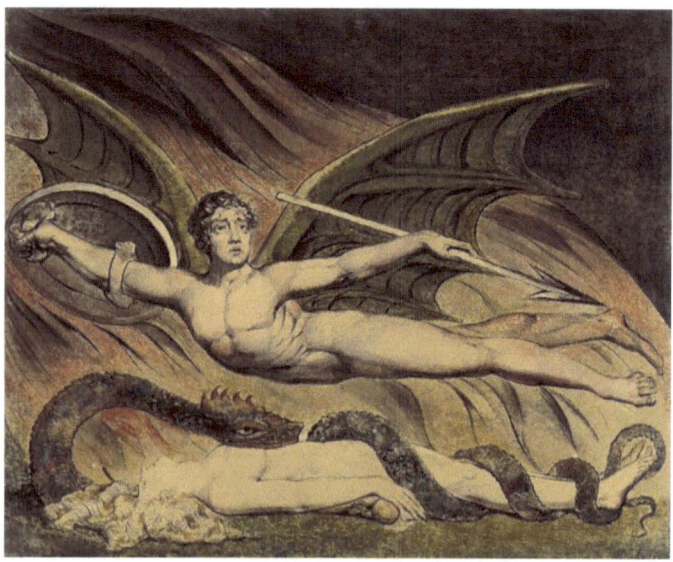

Satan Exulting over Eve, 1795

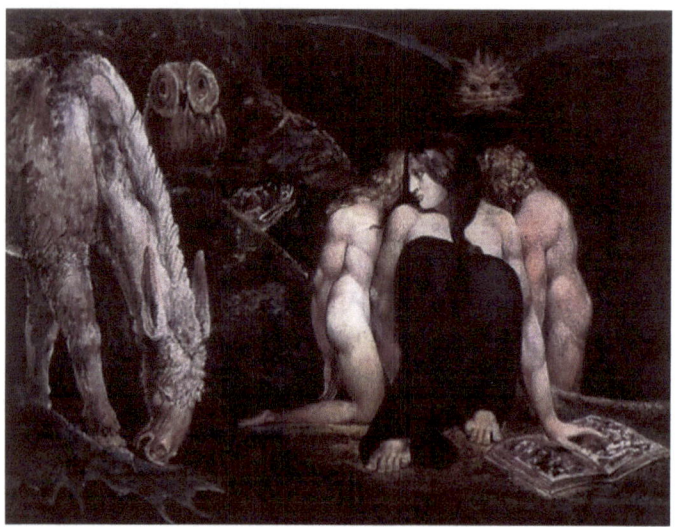

Hecate or the Three Fates

c. 1795, Pen and ink with watercolour, 439 x 581 mm, Tate Gallery, London

Recently the painting is called The Night of Enitharmon's Joy. The many titles show the many levels of meaning, or the impenetrable mystery of Blake's work.

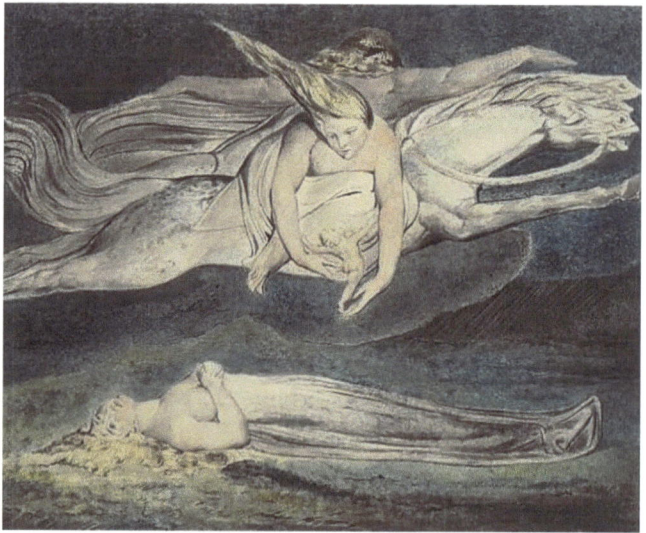

Pity, second impression

1795, Color print finished with pen and ink and watercolor, 42.2 x 52.7 cm, Metropolitan Museum of Art

The existence of a unique proof print (British Museum), in which Blake experimented with his technique on a small scale, suggests that Pity was the first large color print produced by the artist. The child and rider illustrate a double simile from Shakespeare's Macbeth (1:7), in which Macbeth considers the pitiable reaction to his murder of Duncan in terms of vulnerability and vengeance, the human and the supernatural:

And pity, like a naked newborn babe, Striding the blast, or heaven's cherubin horsed Upon the sightless couriers of the air, Shall blow the horrid deed in every eye, That tears shall drown the wind.

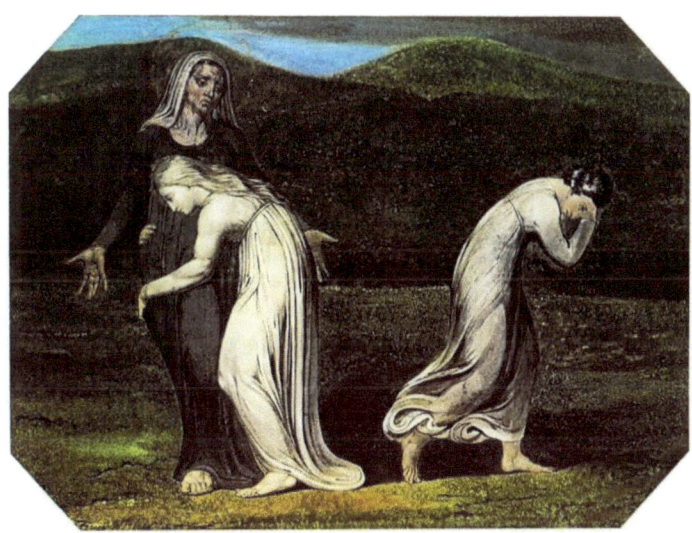

Naomi entreating Ruth and Orpah to return to the land of Moab, 1795

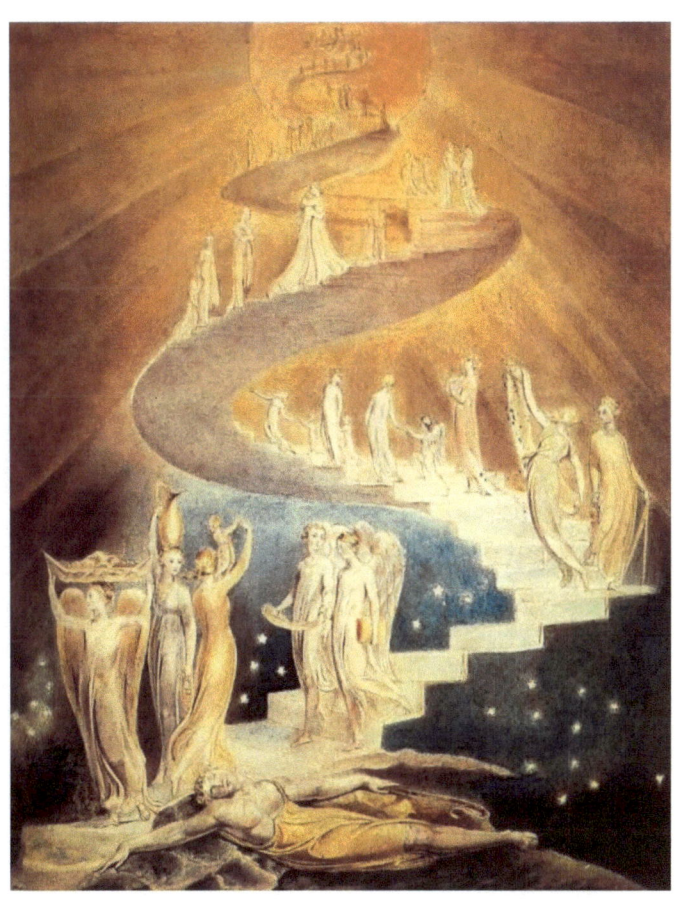

Jacob's Ladder

1799-c.1806, pencil, watercolor

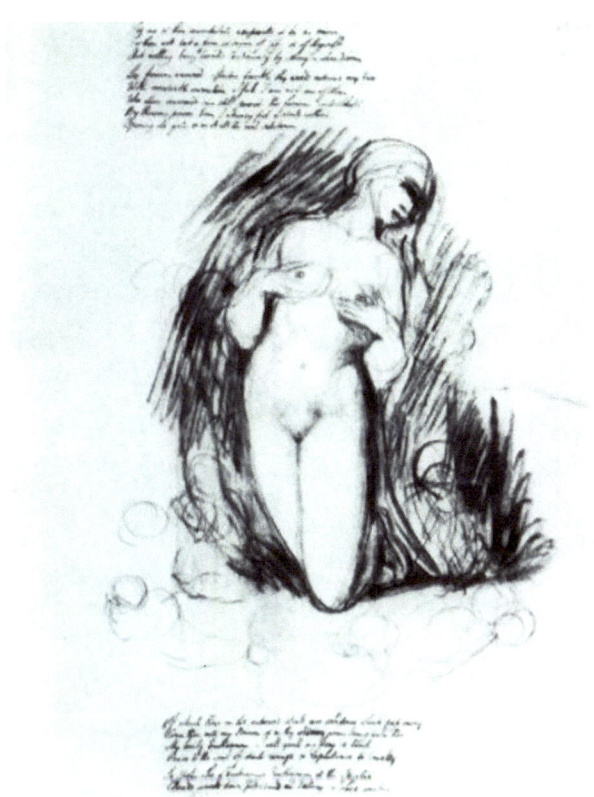

Vala or the Four Zoas

1797-1807, 40.9 × 32 cm, Pencil and chalk, British Museum

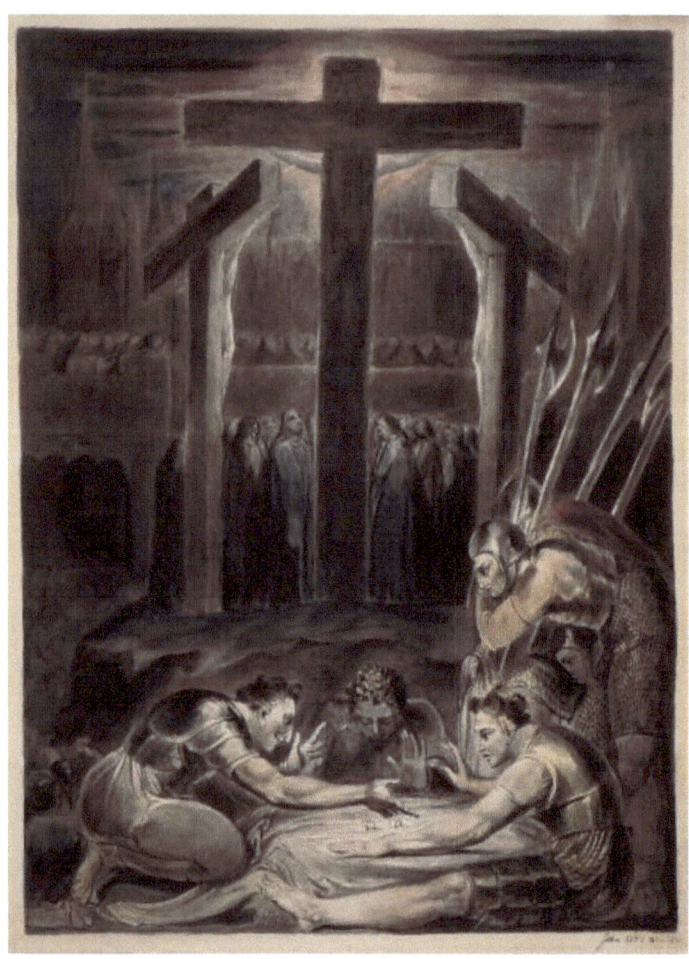

The Soldiers casting lots for Christ's Garments

1800, pen, Indian ink, grey wash and
watercolour on paper, 420 x 314 mm, Fitzwilliam
Museum at the University of Cambridge

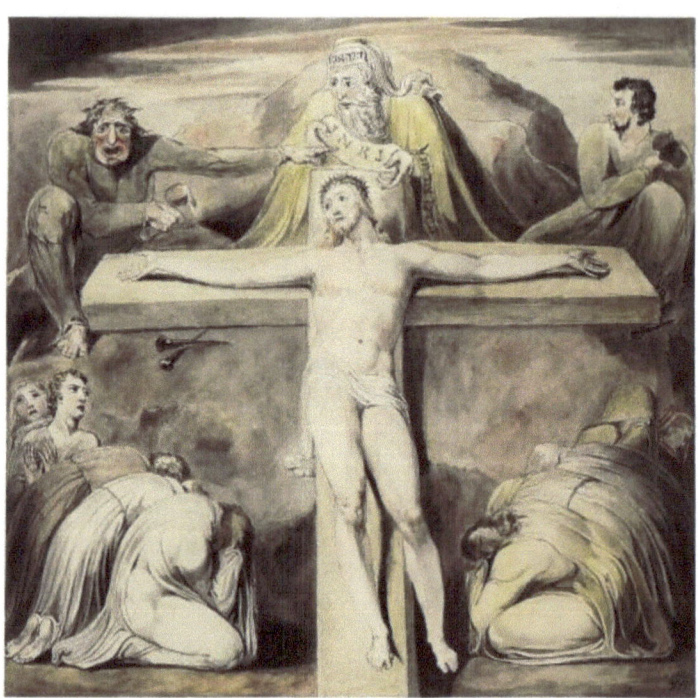

Christ Nailed to the Cross The Third Hour

c.1800-c.1803, pen, ink, watercolor

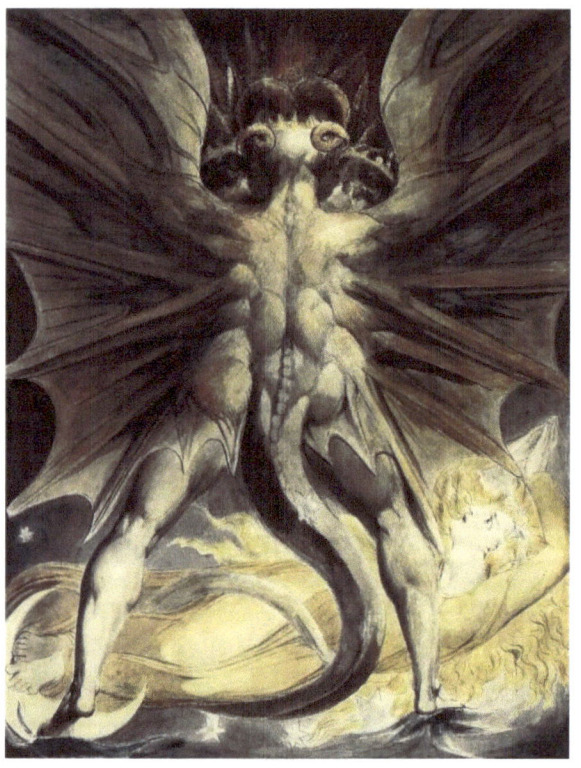

**The Red Dragon and the Woman Clothed with
the Sun**

1803-1805, watercolor

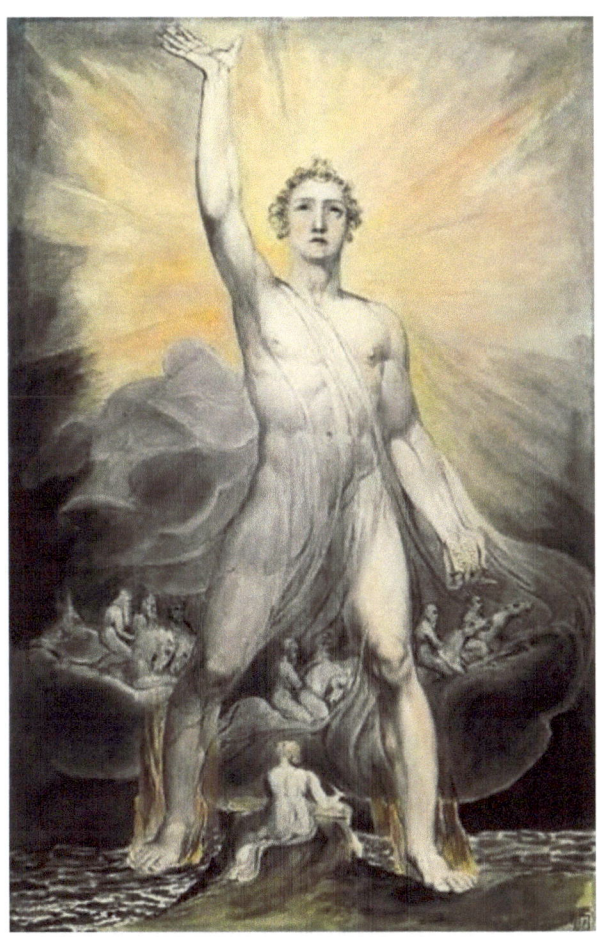

Angel of the Revelation

1803–5, Watercolor, pen and black ink, over traces of graphite, 39.2 x 26 cm, Metropolitan Museum of Art

Blake does not illustrate the biblical text, but its miraculous origin. From his vantage point with the naturalistic foreground space, the diminutive figure of Saint John observes the divine vision that he will later record, embodied in the towering figure of the angel, perhaps inspired by the ancient statue of the Colossus at Rhodes. Indicating the source of his divine text with his heavenward glance and upraised arm, the angel points to the vision that unfolds about his person: above his fiery legs, seven horsemen, presumably embodying the seven thunders of the biblical text, charge through the clouds at the base of his cloak. The subtle coloring, stippled watercolor technique, and extensive pencil underdrawing indicate a date toward the middle of the series.

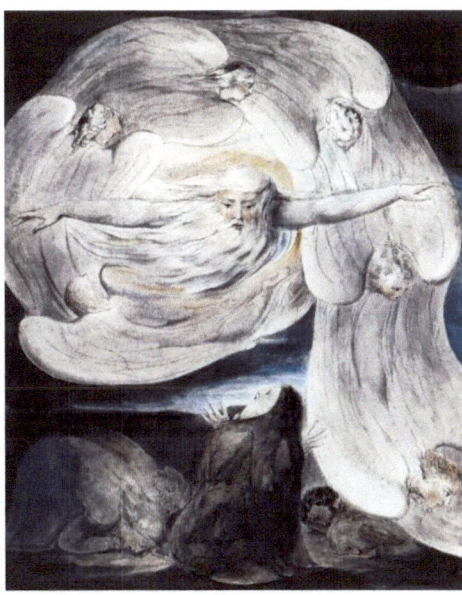

Job Confessing his Presumption to God who Answers from the Whirlwind

1803-05, Pen, ink and watercolour over pencil on paper, 393 x 330 mm, National Gallery of Scotland, Edinburgh

Blake stands alone in the history of British art; his paintings, prints and poetry evoke a private world of religious, mythic and philosophical themes of searing originality. He pursued some conventional training as an apprentice engraver, and briefly as a student at the Royal Academy Schools, but persisted throughout his life with his unorthodox vision. One of the few contemporaries who admired his work was the military clerk Thomas Butts, to whose son Blake gave engraving lessons, and for whom he created over eighty works between 1800 and c. 1809. They treated themes such as the Passion, Apocalyptic beasts and the Old Testament Book of Job, and this watercolour is one of the most splendid. Blake re-visited the subject of Job on a number of occasions, possibly because he identified with Job's trials. Job steadfastly refused to abandon his faith in spite of the numerous misfortunes he had to endure, which included the death of his children and the destruction of his home. Here, at the climax of his torment, surrounded by his prostrated wife and friends, he experiences a mystic vision of God, who, with outstretched arms, is seen amid a vortex of angels. Light appears on the horizon, and Job will be granted redemption.

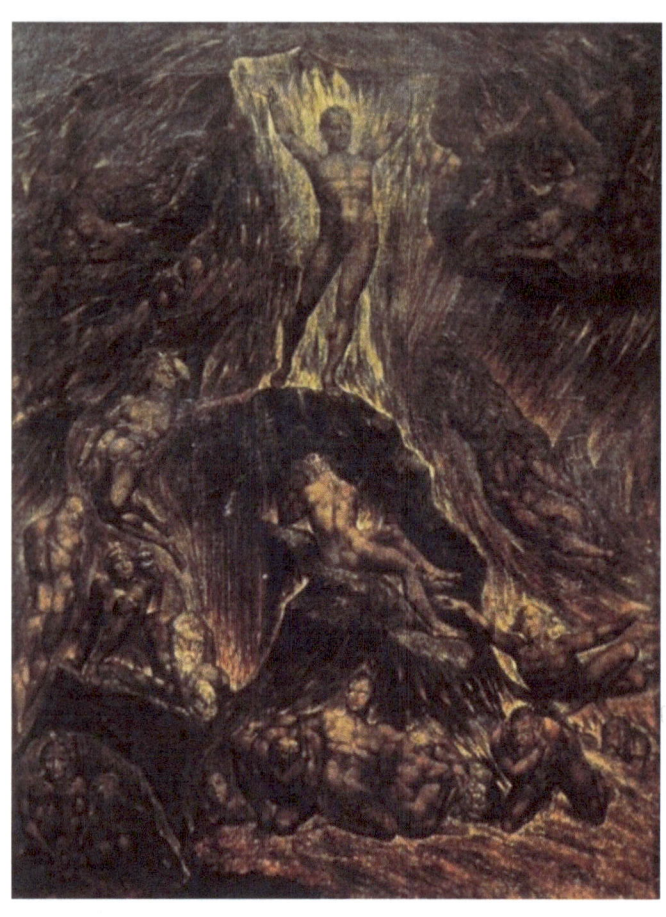

Satan Calling Up his Legions

1804, Pen and ink with watercolour

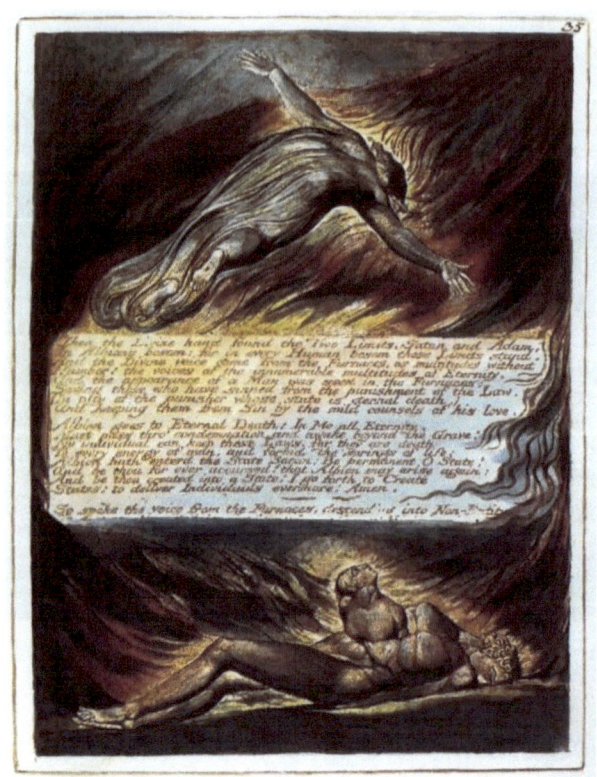

The Descent of Christ

1804-20, Etching with pen, watercolour and gold, 219 x 159 mm, Yale Center for British Art, New Haven

This is Plate 35 of the illustrated poem Jerusalem. In this early page of Jerusalem, the sleeping Albion is visited by Christ, who awakens his dormant desire for salvation. Though Albion is not yet conscious of Christ's sacrifice, its promise is foreshadowed by the new body that begins to emerge from his breast.

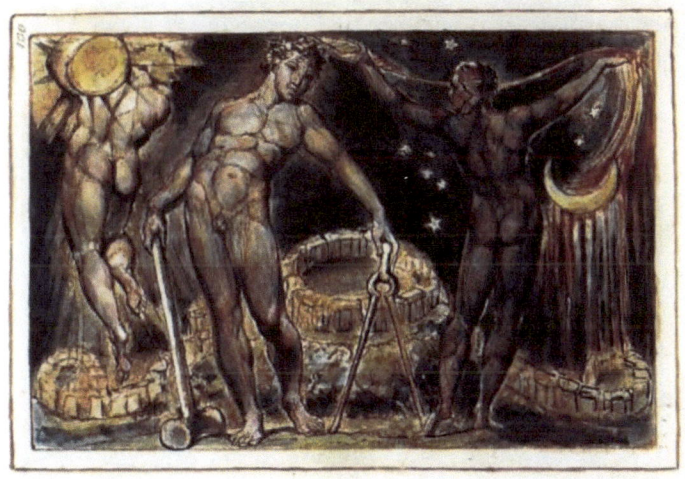

Los

1804-20, Etching with pen, watercolour and gold, 146 x 222 mm, Yale Center for British Art, New Haven

This is Plate 100 of the illustrated poem Jerusalem. Trained as an engraver, Blake evolved into a shamanic figure - mystic, philosopher, priest - compelled to set his visions before the world. They took the form of epic, quasi-biblical dramas of spiritual redemption. He increasingly eschewed conventional media and published them in 'Prophetic Books' written and illuminated himself by processes of colour printing. In his Prophetic Books, the character of Los exemplifies the artist's roles as seer, mystic and interpreter. The author of all art and literature, architect of a City of Art, Los is responsible for everything mankind sees and senses. In Jerusalem he takes various forms, from a London nightwatchman to a blacksmith at his forge, but he is also Blake himself. When the narrative reaches its last page, Los rests from his smithy, but a temple of false religion is already extending to cover the land behind him as night follows day.

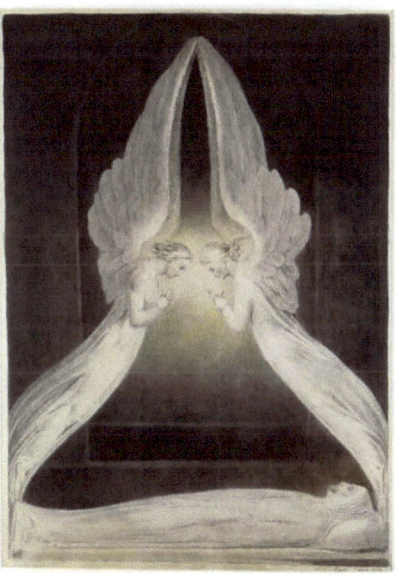

The Angels hovering over the body of Christ in the Sepulchre; Christ in the sepulchre, guarded by angels

1805, Watercolour, pen and ink, Victoria and Albert Museum

This drawing depicts the body of Jesus Christ, which was placed in a cave (his tomb or sepulchre) following his death by crucifixion. When Mary Magdalene visits, she is startled to find two angels sitting at the head and feet 'where the body of Jesus had lain'. Jesus then appears and speaks to her. For his imagery Blake sought out a description in the Book of Exodus in the Old Testament, which recounts the history of the Jews many centuries before Jesus Christ lived. When the prophet Moses is alone on Mount Sinai, Jehovah tells him to instruct the Israelites to make a 'mercy seat' flanked by cherubims (angels) all made of gold. The description of the angels in Exodus is the source for Blake's design. It was in Moses' day that a monotheistic religion was established for the Israelites, and that fact plus Mary Magdalene's account of the two angels in the sepulchre, has made for many the Exodus moment a prefiguration of a founding moment of the Christian religion. This drawing depicts a scene from the Book of Exodus in the Old Testament. This is an unusual and striking visual interpretation of the biblical text. The strange light and colours used here convey a sense of the mystery of the scene.

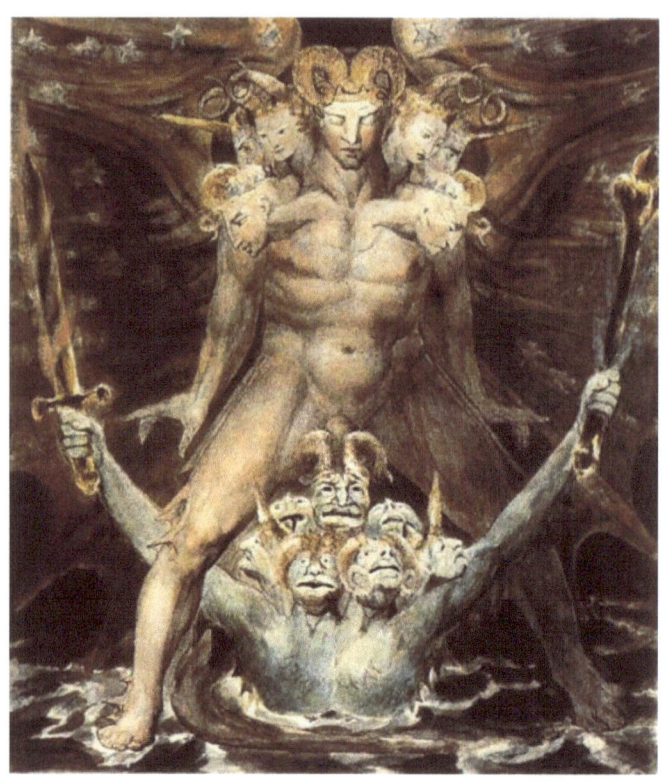

The Great Red Dragon and the Beast from the Sea

1805, Pen and ink with watercolor

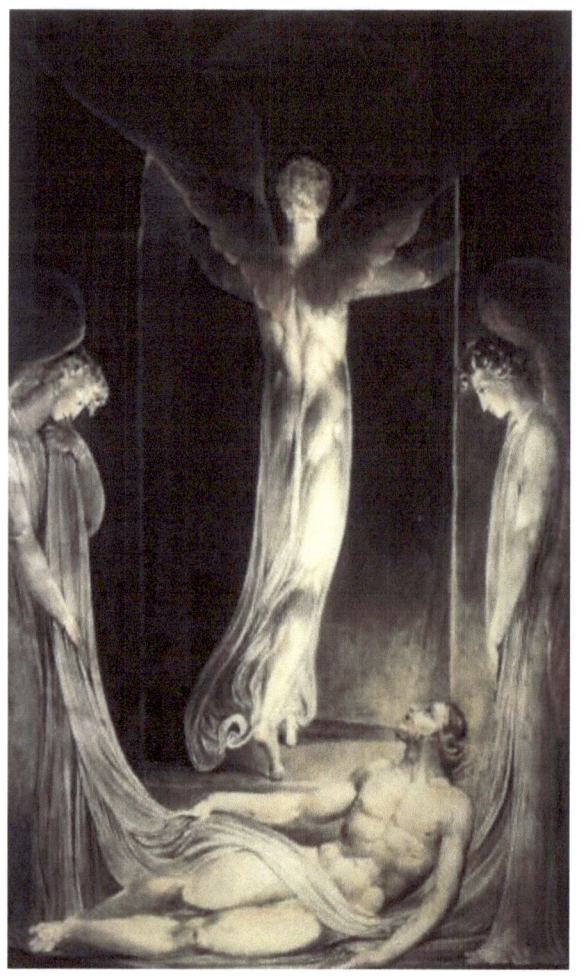

The Resurrection

c. 1805, Pen, ink, watercolour, 412 x 300 mm,
Victoria and Albert Museum, London

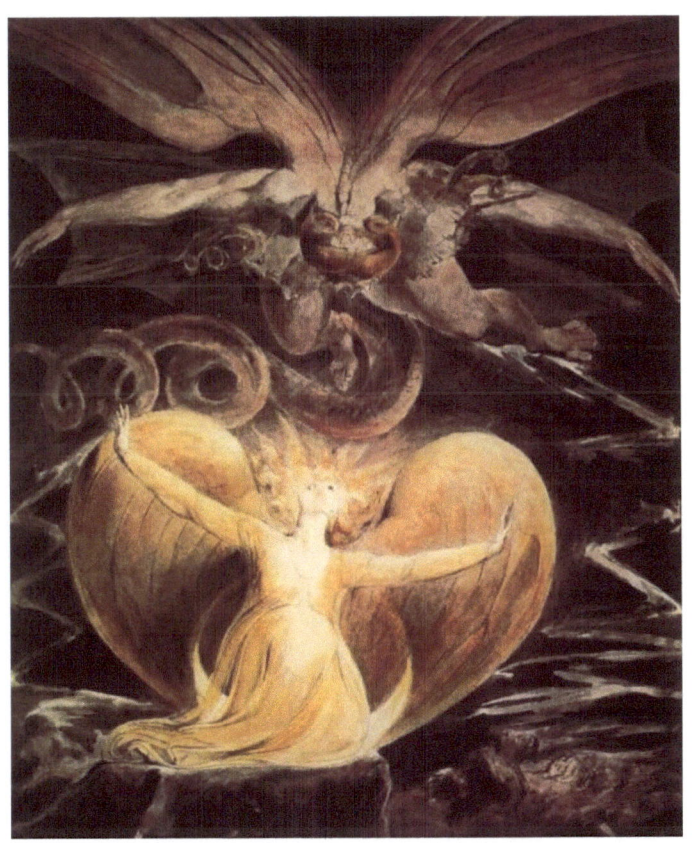

The Great Red Dragon and the Woman clothed with the sun

1805-1810, Pen and ink with watercolor

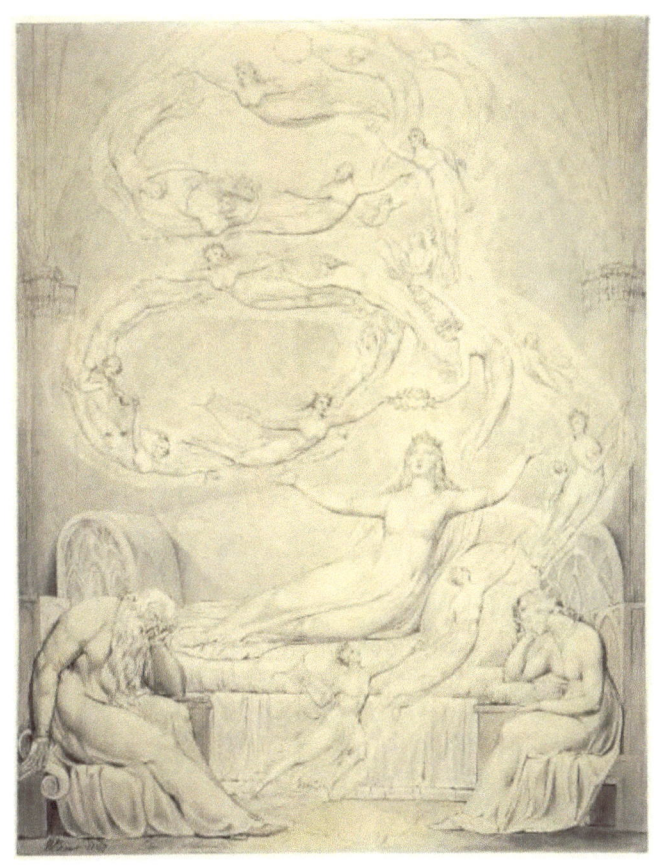

Queen Katherine's Dream

1807, pen, grey wash, traces of graphite underdrawing, touched with colour paper, 399 x 314 mm, Fitzwilliam Museum at the University of Cambridge

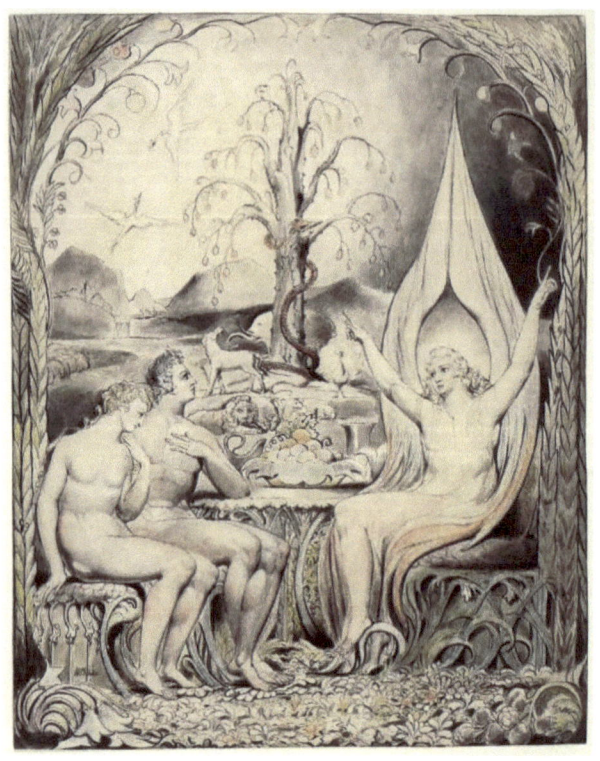

Illustration to Milton`s Paradise Lost

1807, watercolor

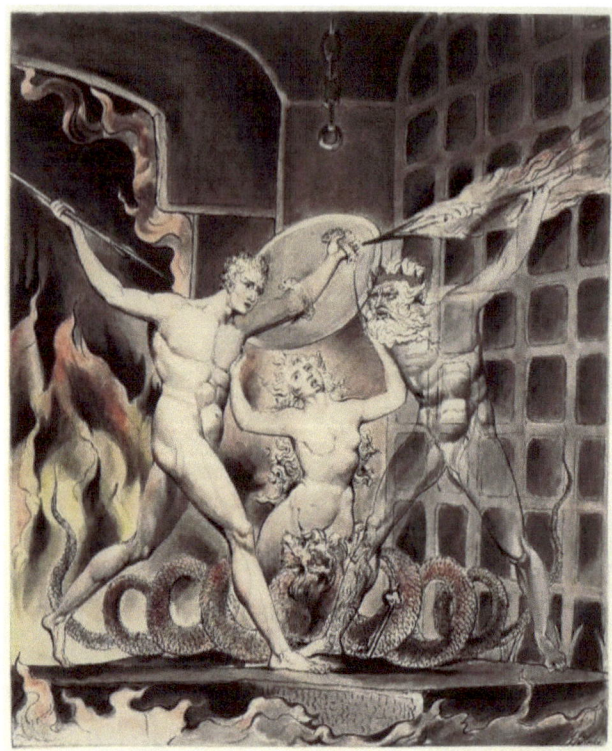

Illustration to Milton`s Paradise Lost

1807, watercolor

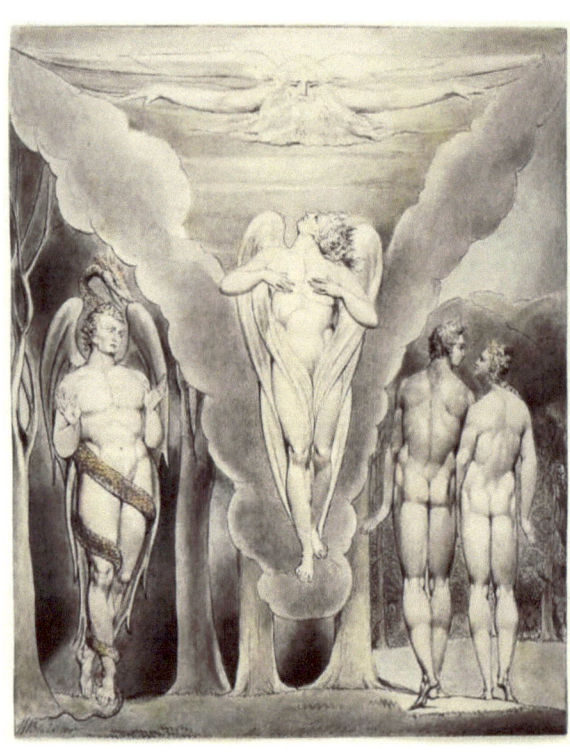

Illustration to Milton`s Paradise Lost

1807, watercolor

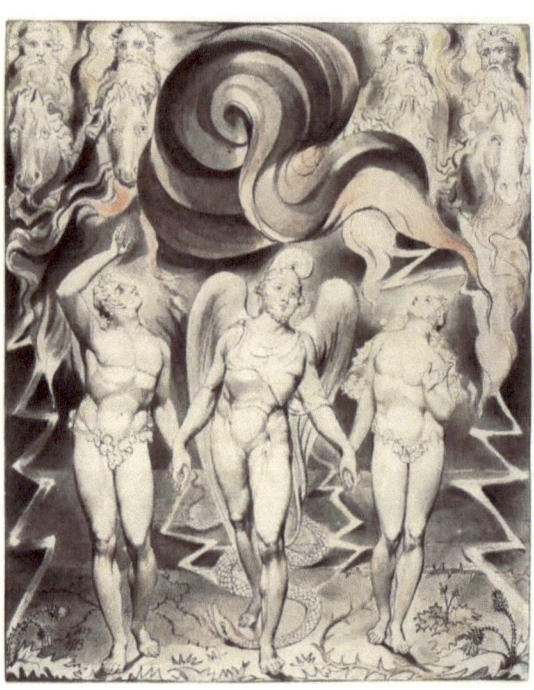

Illustration to Milton`s Paradise Lost

1807, watercolor

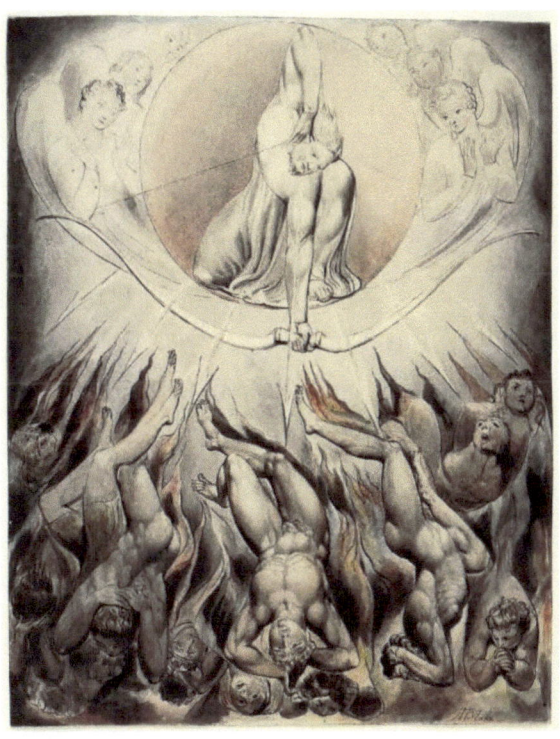

Illustration to Milton`s Paradise Lost

1807, watercolor

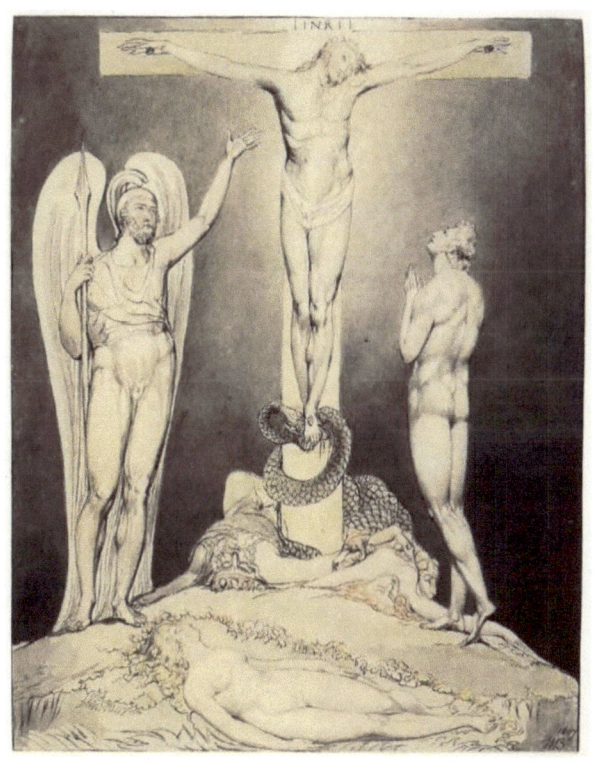

Illustration to Milton`s Paradise Lost, 1807,
watercolor

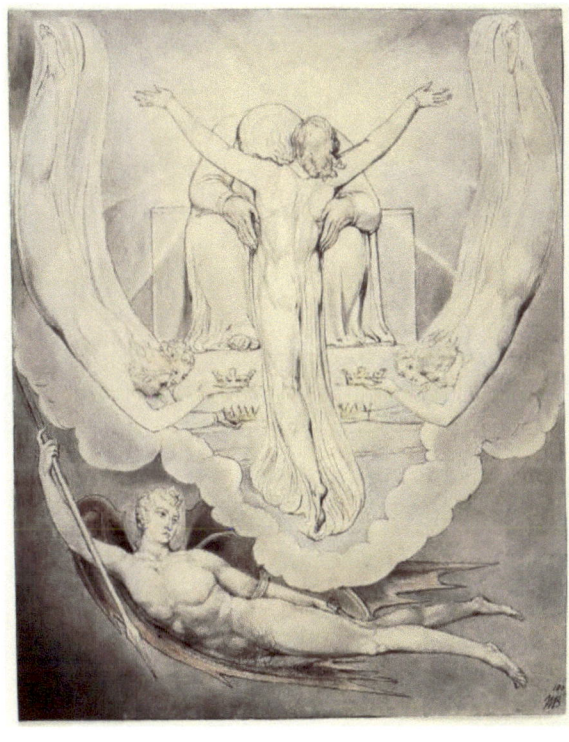

Illustration to Milton`s Paradise Lost

1807, watercolor

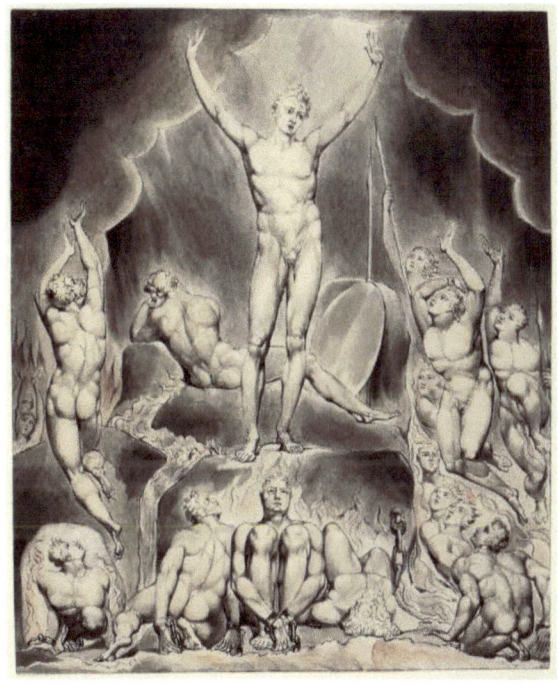

Illustration to Milton`s Paradise Lost

1807, watercolor

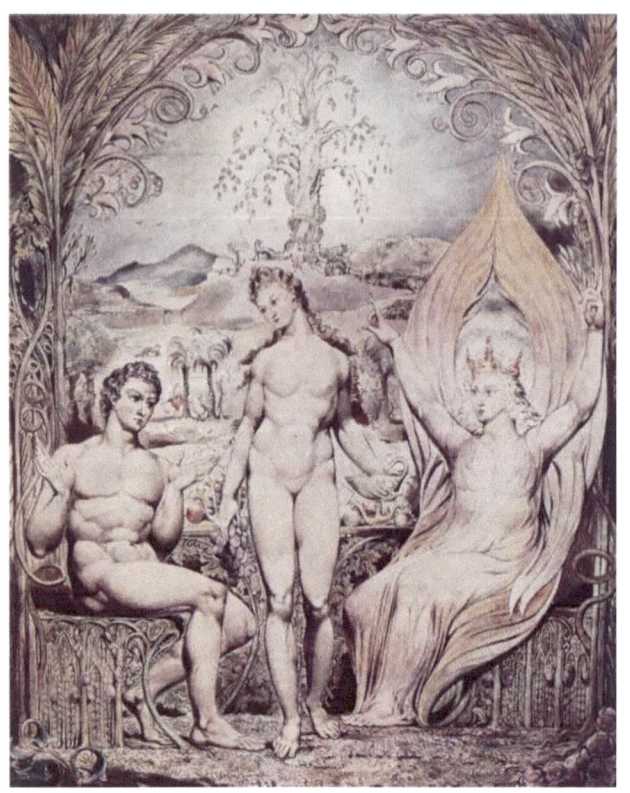

Archangel Raphael with Adam and Eve, 1808

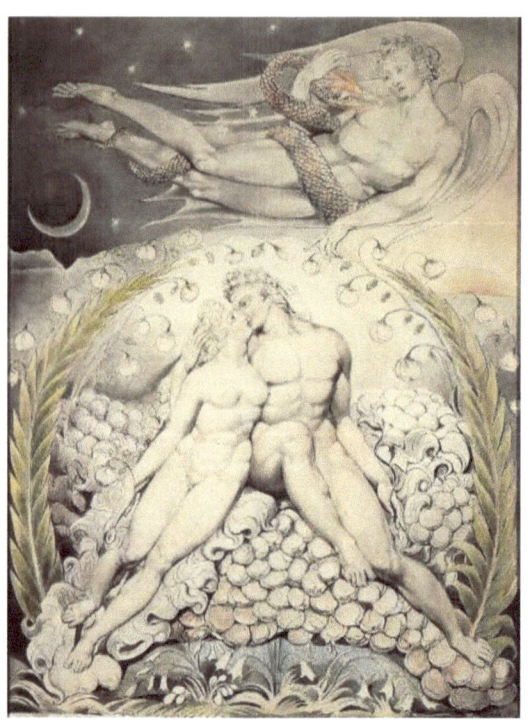

Satan Watching the Caresses of Adam and Eve

1808, Pen and watercolor on paper, 505 x 380 mm, Museum of Fine Arts, Boston

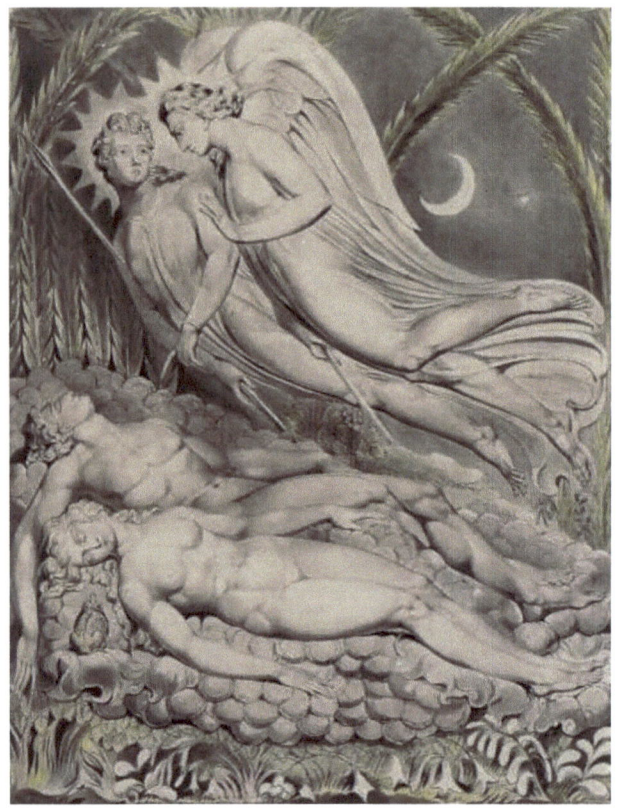

Adam and Eve Sleeping

1808, Pen and watercolor on paper, 492 x 387 mm, Museum of Fine Arts, Boston

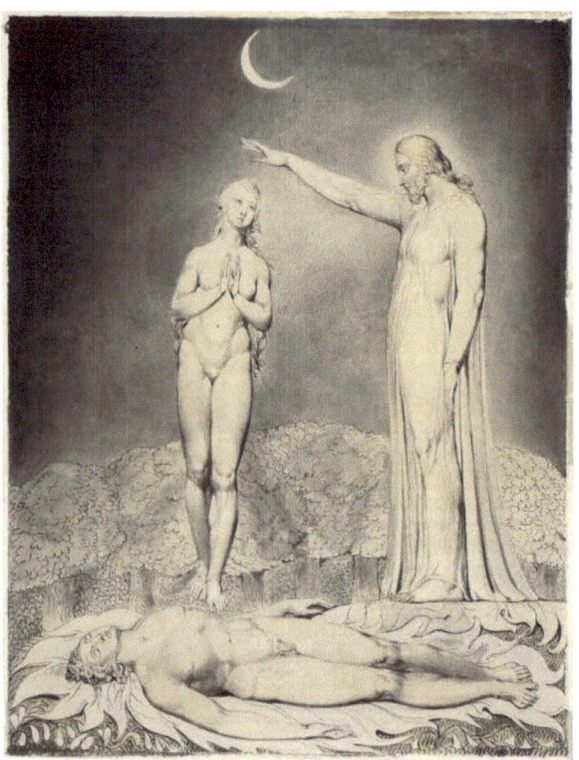

Illustration to Milton`s Paradise Lost, 1808

18

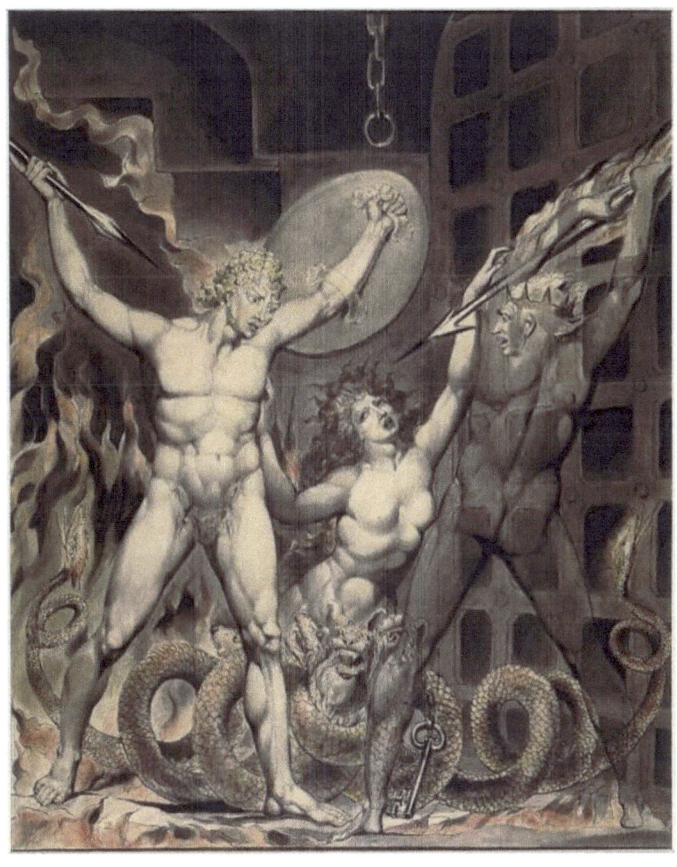

Illustration to Milton`s Paradise Lost, 1808

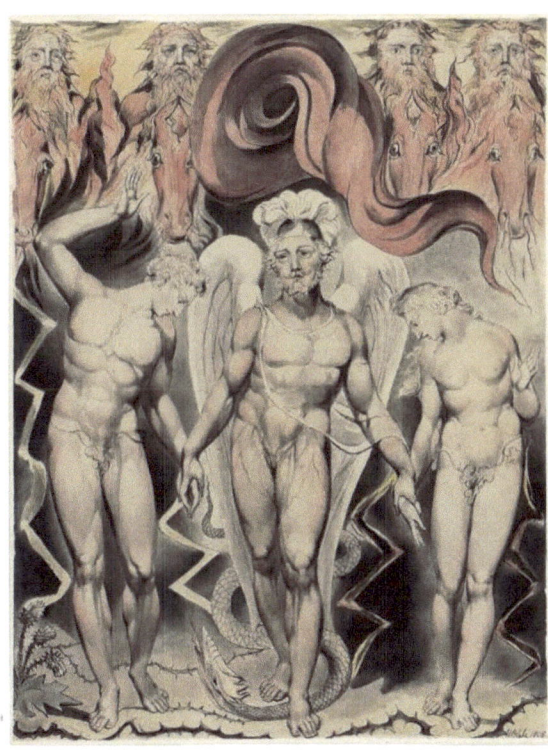

Illustration to Milton`s Paradise Lost, 1808

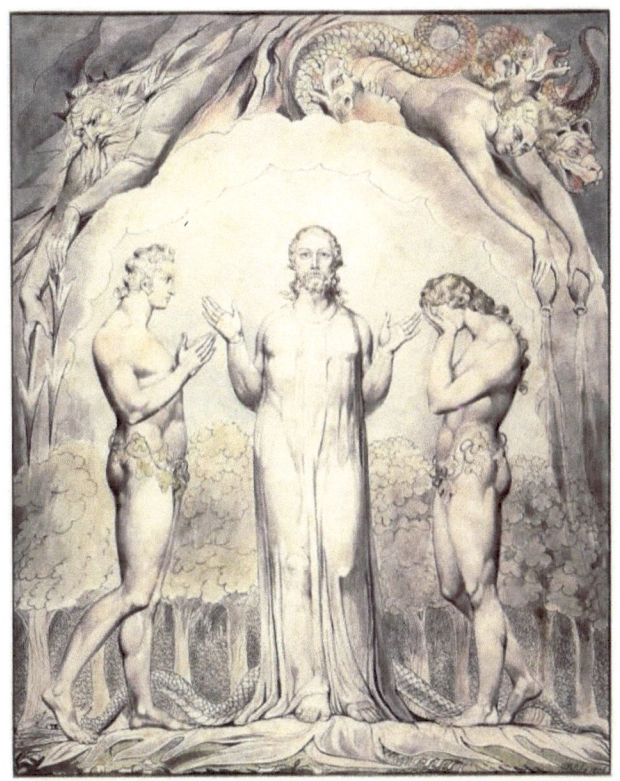

Illustration to Milton`s Paradise Lost, 1808

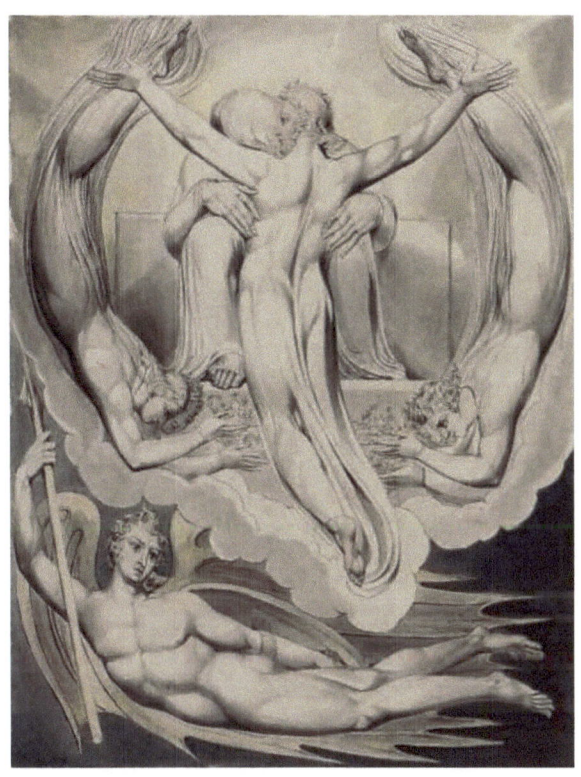

Christ as the Redeemer of Man

1808, Pen and watercolour, 496 x 393 mm,
Museum of Fine Arts, Boston

Blake's visionary drawing style is demonstrated in this illustration to Milton's Paradise Lost, III. Christ floats in the air before God the Father, the position of his body referring to his death on the cross. The expressive, outsized hands of his father touch him lightly. Four angels accompany Christ on his way to Earth. The unremitting movement contains tension. Even in terms of colour the divine realm is divided from the void, in which Satan, armed with a spear, attempts to prevent God's plan of redemption for the world. The scene is characterized by symmetry and repetition, and is not only illuminated by the artist's technique, but is also enlightened spiritually.

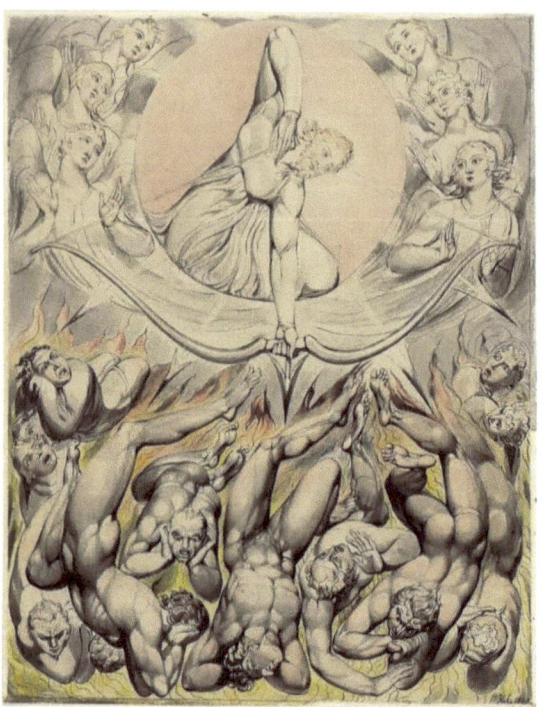

The Casting of the Rebel Angels into Hell

1808, watercolor

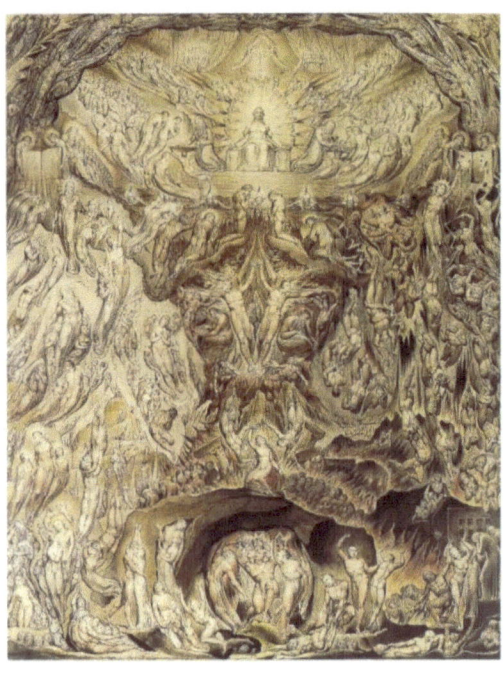

Last Judgement, 1808, pen, watercolor

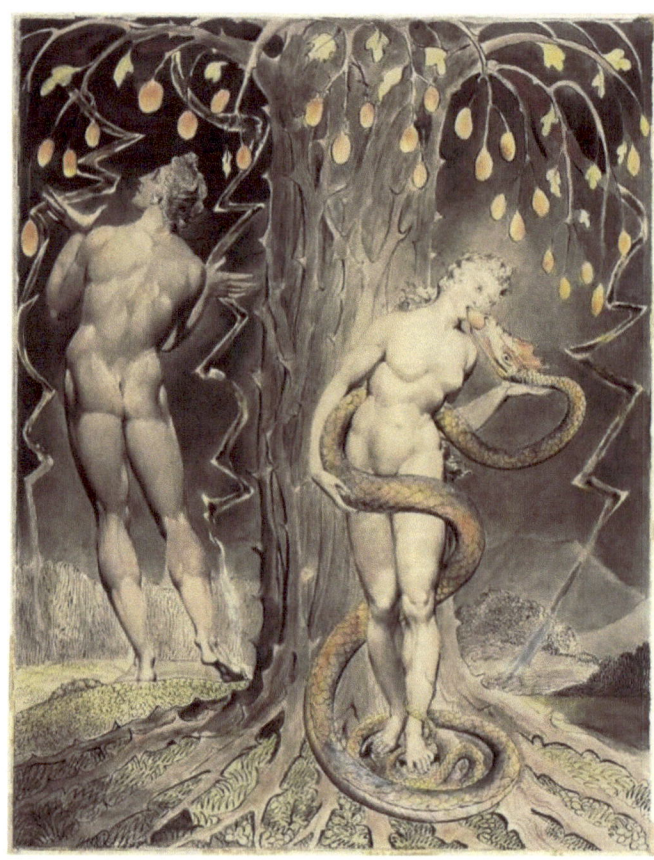

The Temptation and Fall of Eve, 1808

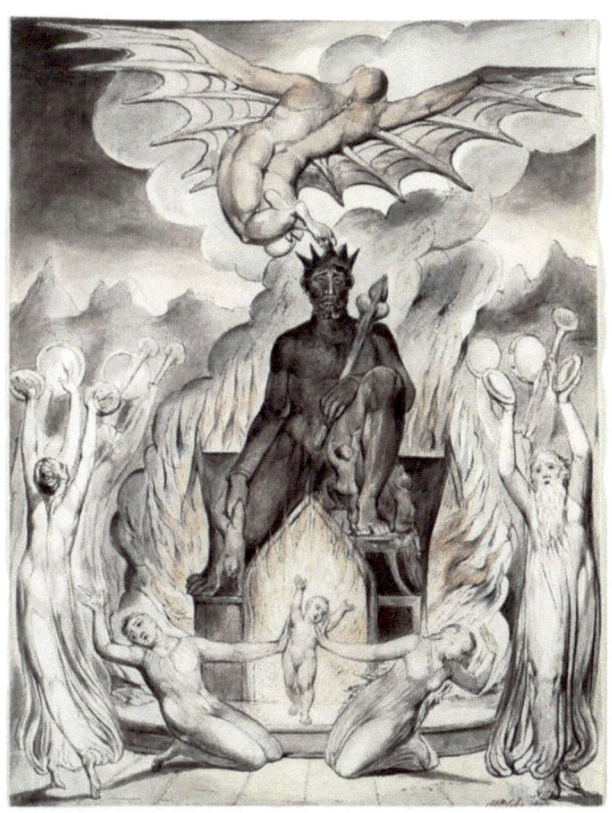

Illustration to Milton`s On the Morning of Christ`s Nativity, 1809

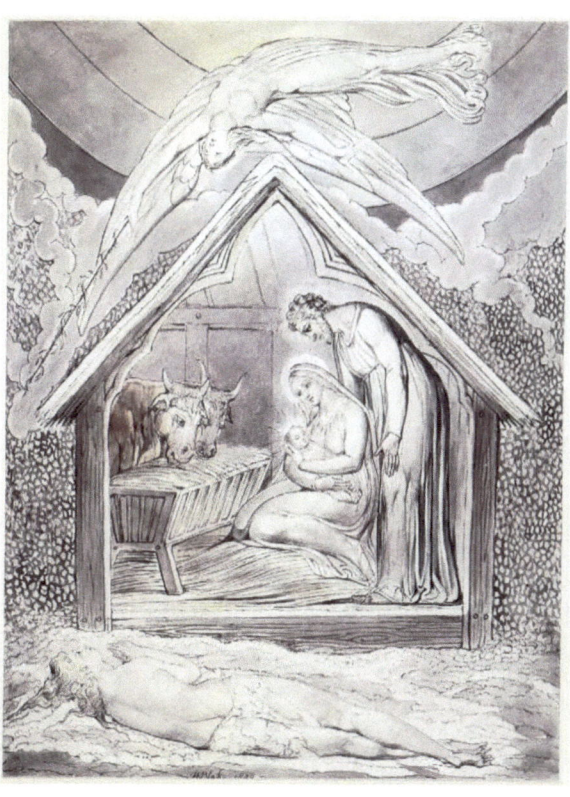

Illustration to Milton`s On the Morning of Christ`s Nativity, 1809

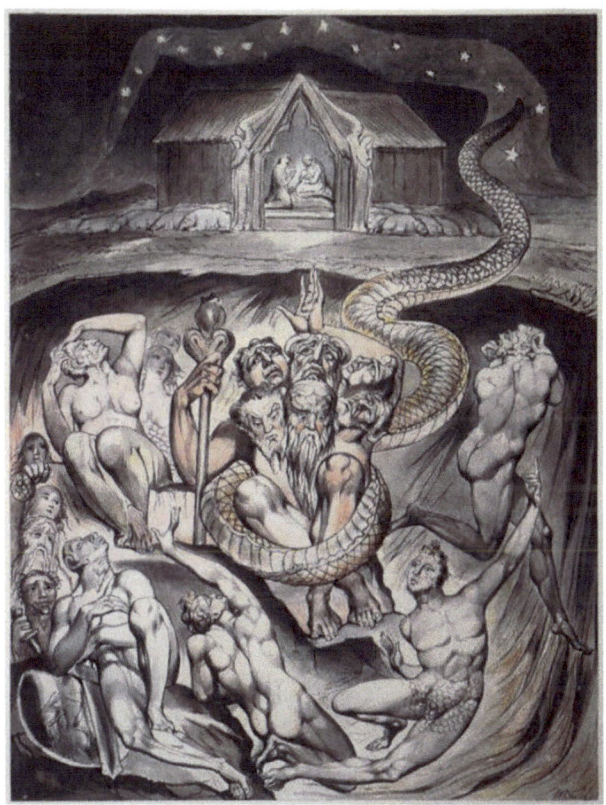

Illustration to Milton`s On the Morning of Christ`s Nativity, 1809

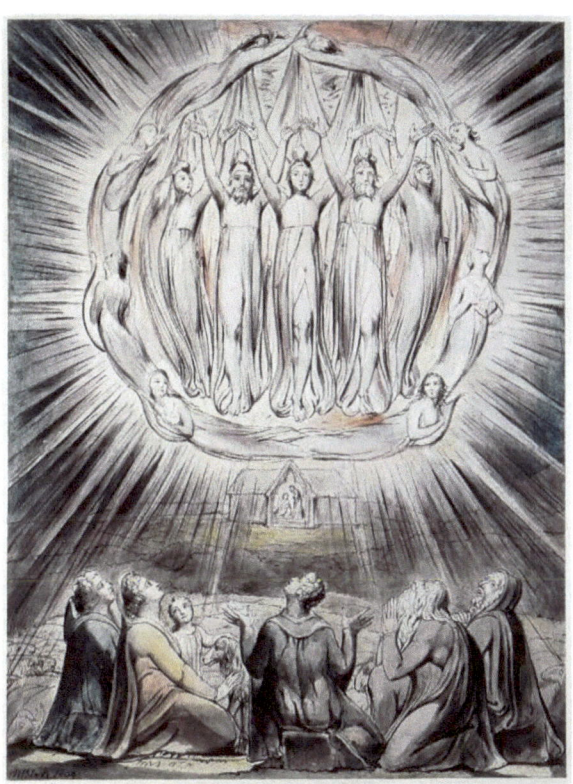

Illustration to Milton`s On the Morning of Christ`s Nativity, 1809

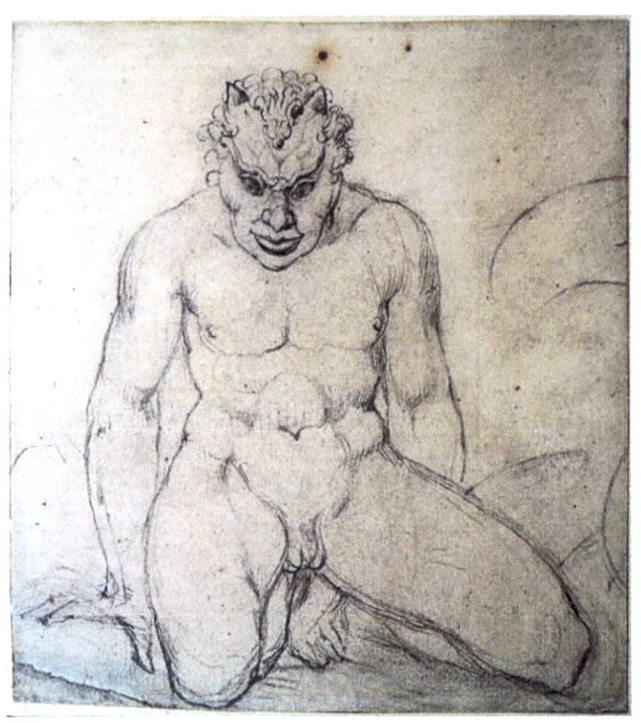

A Squatted Devil with Young Horns

1810, Pencil on paper, Private collection.

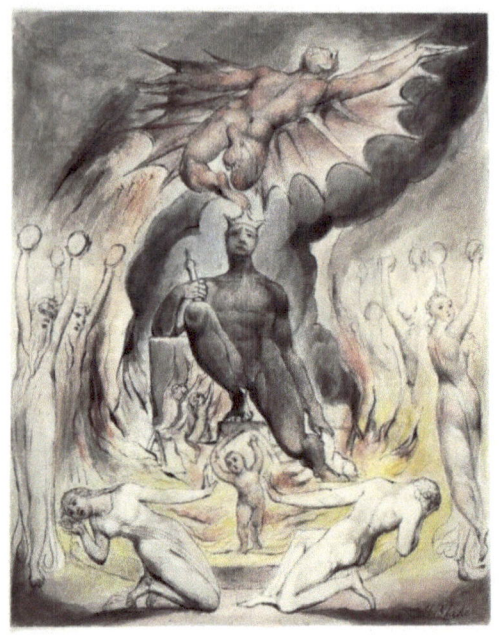

Illustration to Milton`s On the Morning of Christ`s Nativity, 1815

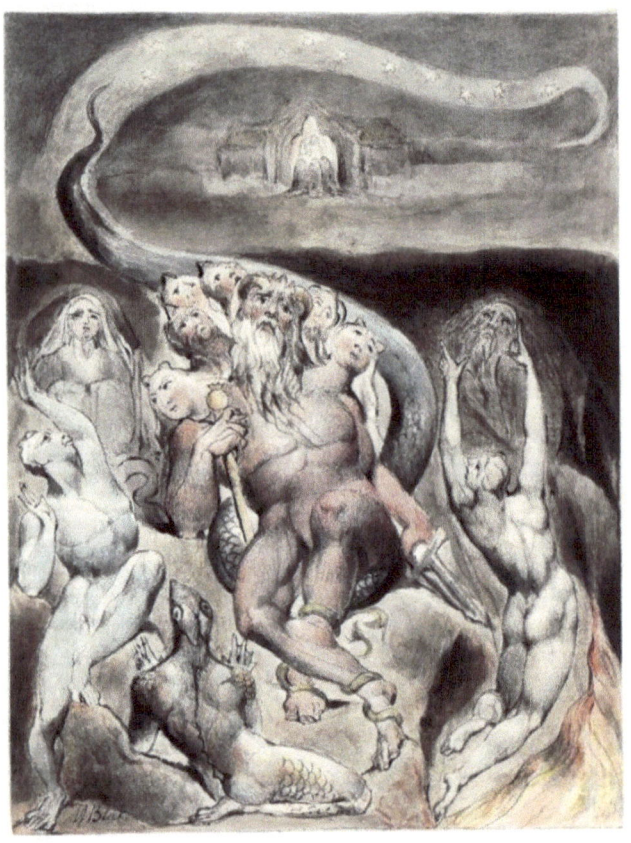

Illustration to Milton`s On the Morning of Christ`s Nativity, 1815

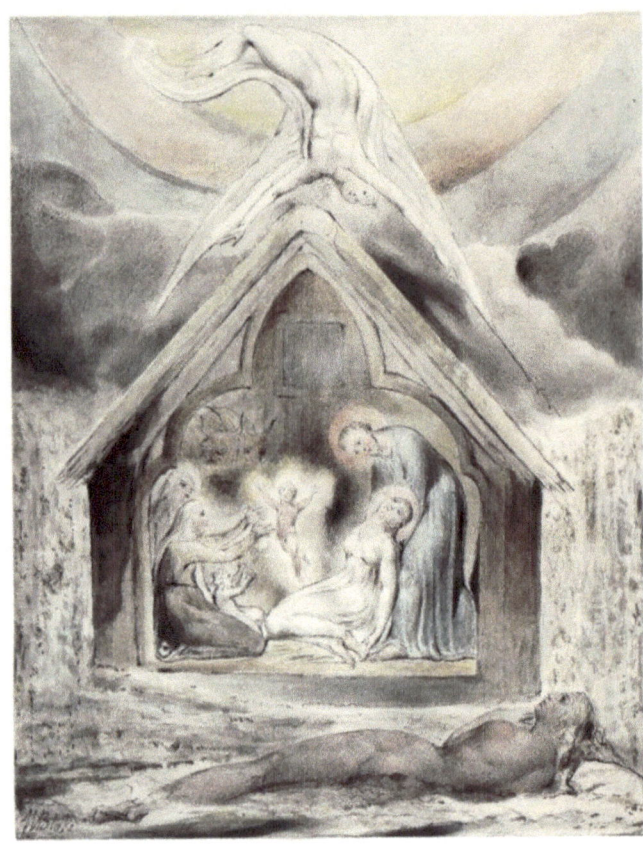

The Night of Peace, 1815

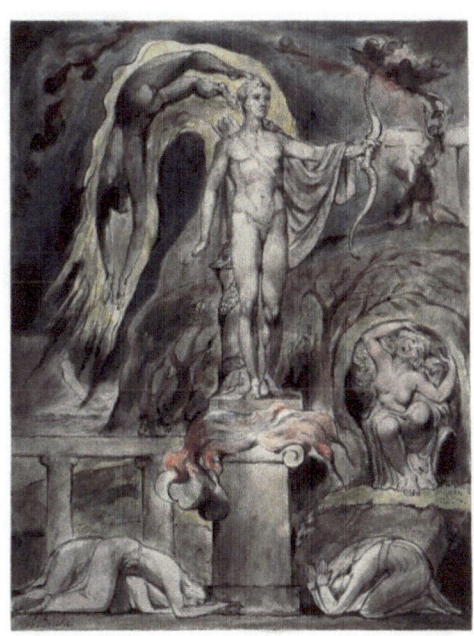

The Shrine of Apollo: Milton's Hymn on the Morning of Christ's Nativity, 1815

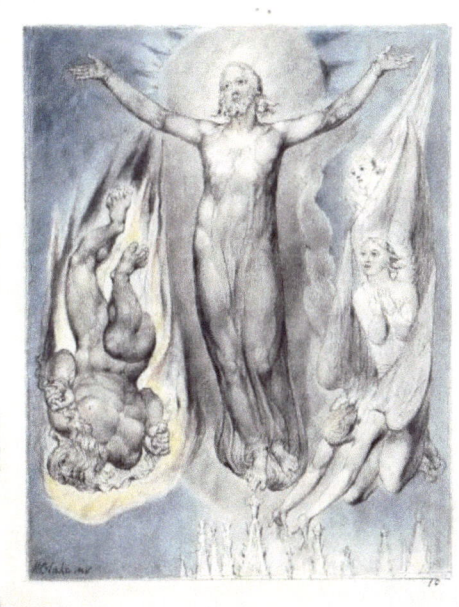

**Christ placed on the pinnacle of the Temple
Paradise Regained**

1818, pen, Indian ink, grey wash and watercolour on paper, 166 x 133 mm, Fitzwilliam Museum at the University of Cambridge

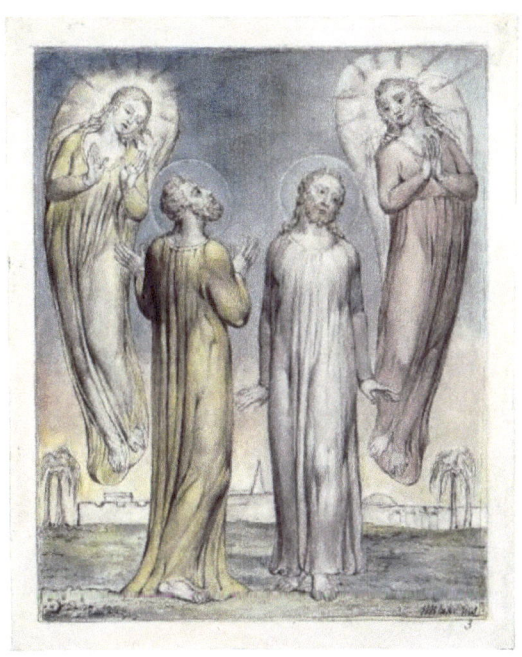

**Andrew and Simon Peter searching for Christ
Paradise Regained**

1818, pen, Indian ink, grey wash and watercolour on paper, 190 x 138 mm, Fitzwilliam Museum at the University of Cambridge

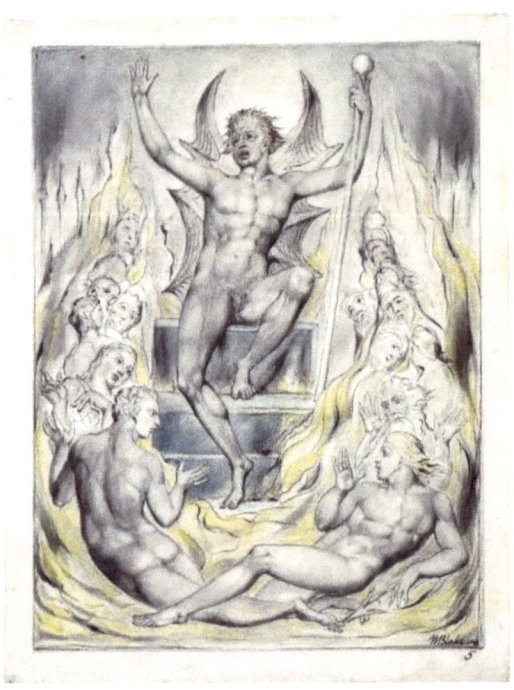

Satan addressing his potentates Paradise Regained

1818., graphite, Indian ink, and colour washes on paper, 173 x 133 mm, Fitzwilliam Museum at the University of Cambridge

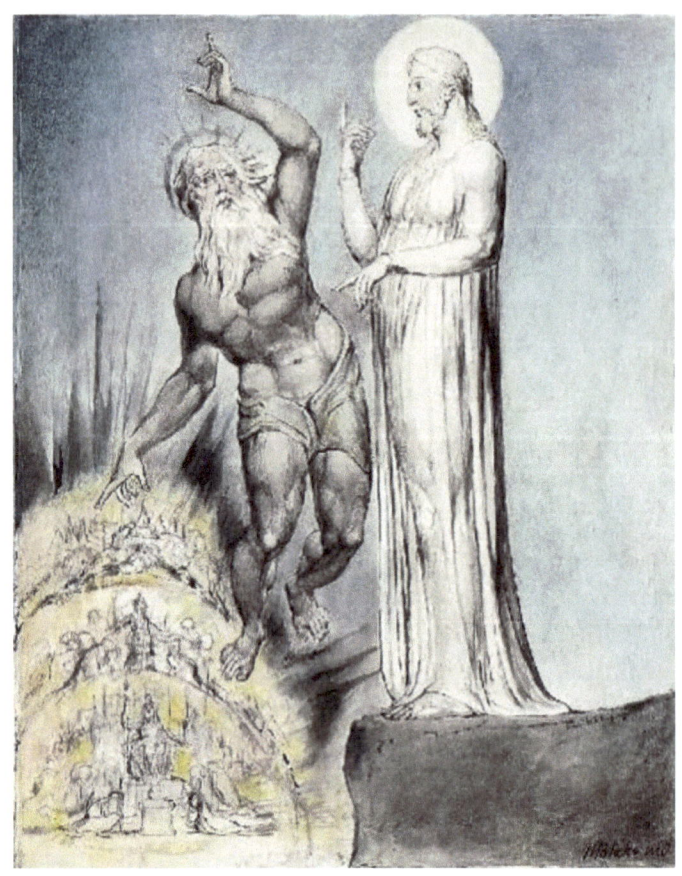

Satan tempts Christ with the Kingdoms of the Earth Paradise Regained

1818, graphite, Indian ink, and colour washes on paper, 168 x 131 mm, Fitzwilliam Museum at the University of Cambridge

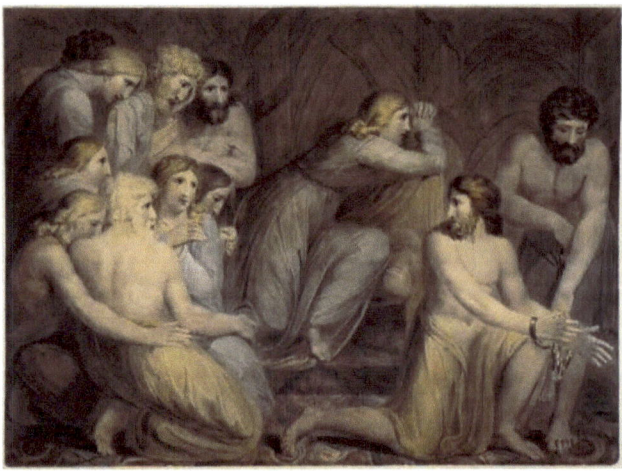

Joseph ordering Simeon to be bound The Story of Joseph

1818, Indian ink and watercolour over graphite on paper, 405 x 560 mm, Fitzwilliam Museum at the University of Cambridge

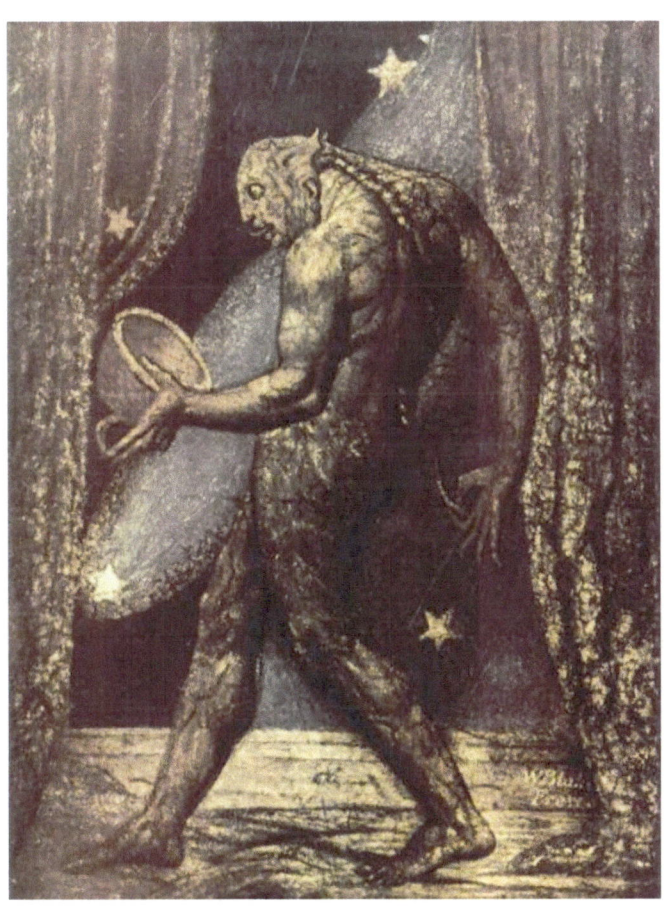

The Ghost of a Flea, 1819-1820, tempera

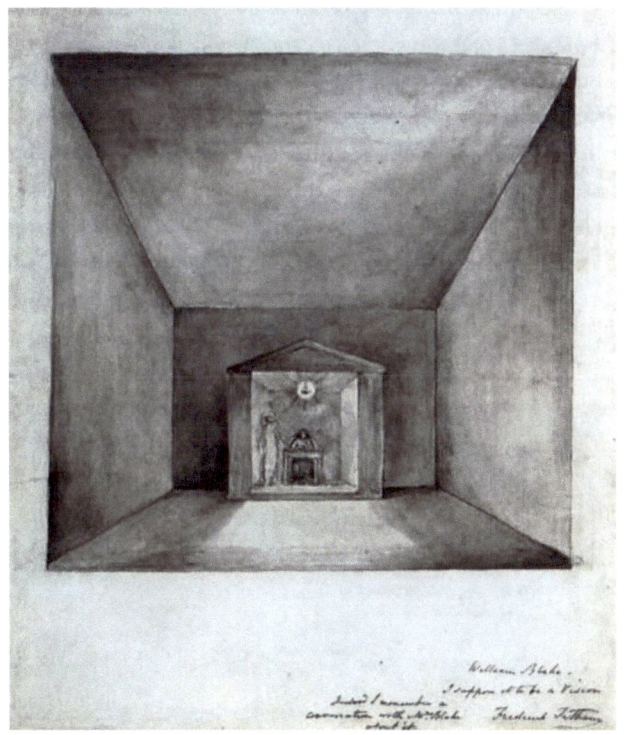

Elisha in the Chamber on the Wall

c. 1820, Sepia washes over pencil, 243 x 210 mm,
Tate Gallery, London

Among Blake's metaphors for creative vision
was the Old Testament prophet Elisha,
foretelling her future son to the Shunammite
woman who had given him a room for his
meditations. There can be little doubt that
Blake's bearded seer in his chamber was a more
revealing record of himself and his art than a
literal portrayal of his features could ever be.

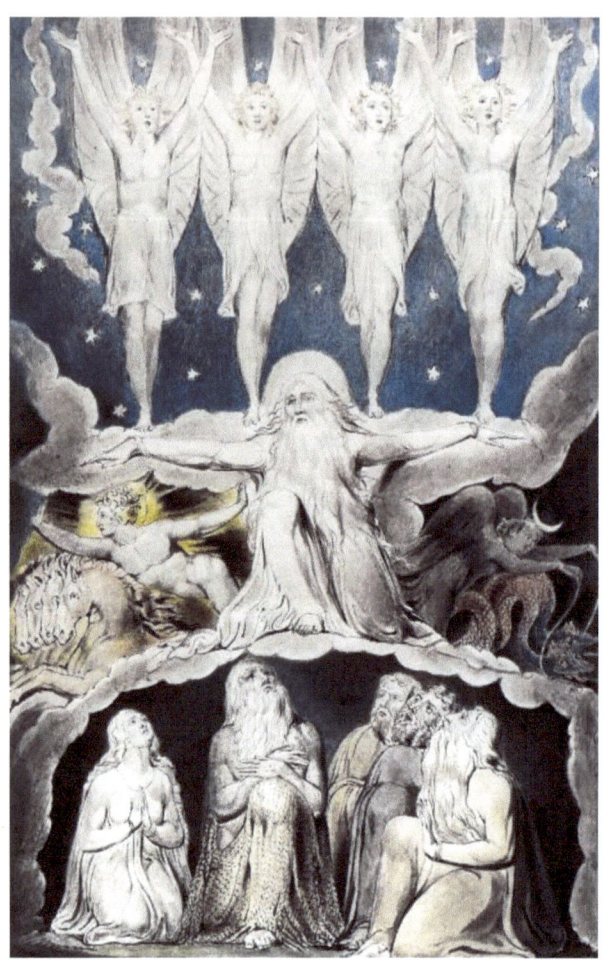

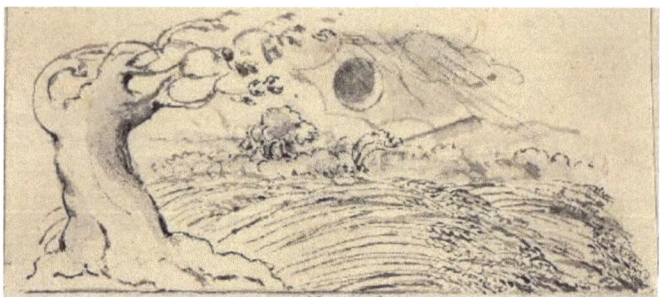

The Blighted Corn

1820, graphite, pen and grey wash on paper, 41 x 96 mm, Fitzwilliam Museum at the University of Cambridge

The Book of Job: When the Morning Stars Sang Together

1820, Watercolour, 280 x 179 mm, The Morgan Library and Museum, New York

Blake's images oscillate between dream and reason. Even direct references to the Bible, as here to the Book of Job, do not necessarily mean that this is an illustration of the Bible. The scenes are too much a part of the artist's private religious vision. Here we see Job, who has been through torment and suffering, taken up by God. With His arms outstretched, God appears as the Lord of Light and Darkness, but the depiction could also be intended to show God as the Lord of the Earth. There is a striking similarity in the faces of God and Job.

The sheet is a drawing for one of the sequences of engravings that appeared from 1825.

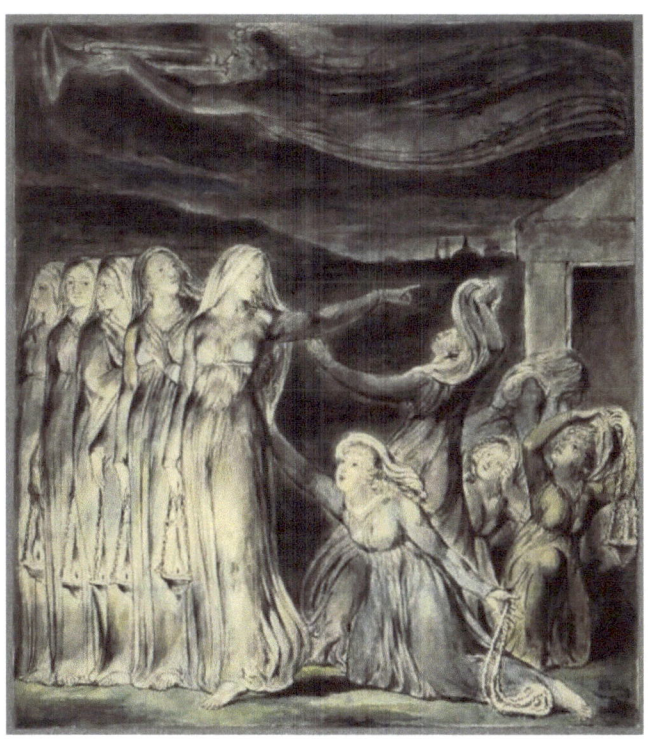

The Parable of the Wise and Foolish Virgins

1822, pen, Indian ink, grey wash and watercolour on paper, 363 x 337 mm, Fitzwilliam Museum at the University of Cambridge

The Parable of the Wise and Foolish Virgins—a call to live in anticipation of the final day of reckoning and salvation (from Matthew 25:1–13)—contrasts five maidens who have prepared for the arrival of their bridegrooms by obtaining oil for their lamps with five others who have squandered their opportunity and therefore miss their marriage feasts. This elegant watercolor, composed within a single plane resembling a classical low-relief sculpture, is the earliest of four versions of the subject to be painted by Blake.

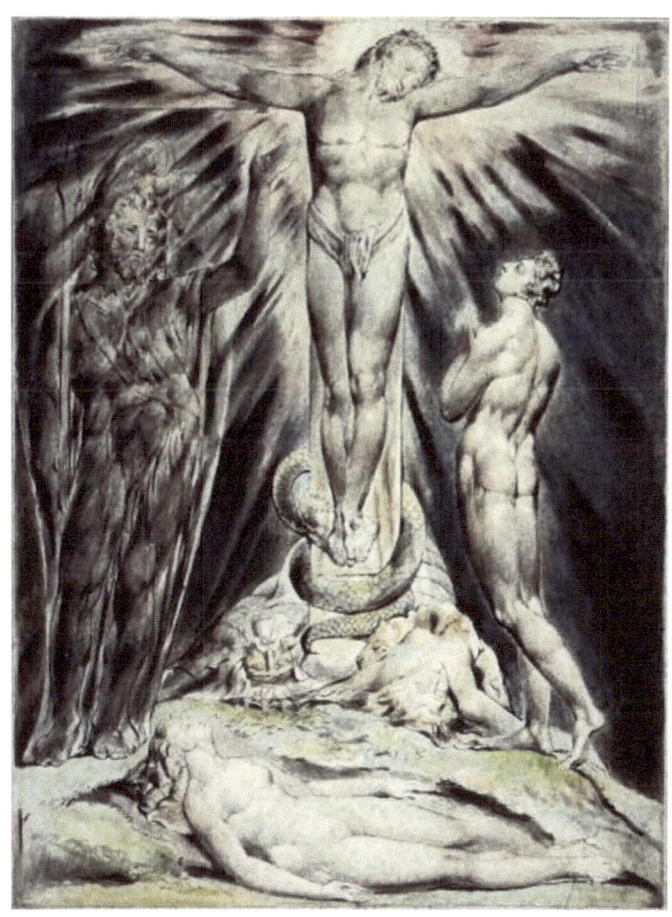

The Archangel Michael Foretelling the Crucifixion

1822, pen, Indian ink, grey wash and watercolour on paper, 502 x 385 mm, Fitzwilliam Museum at the University of Cambridge

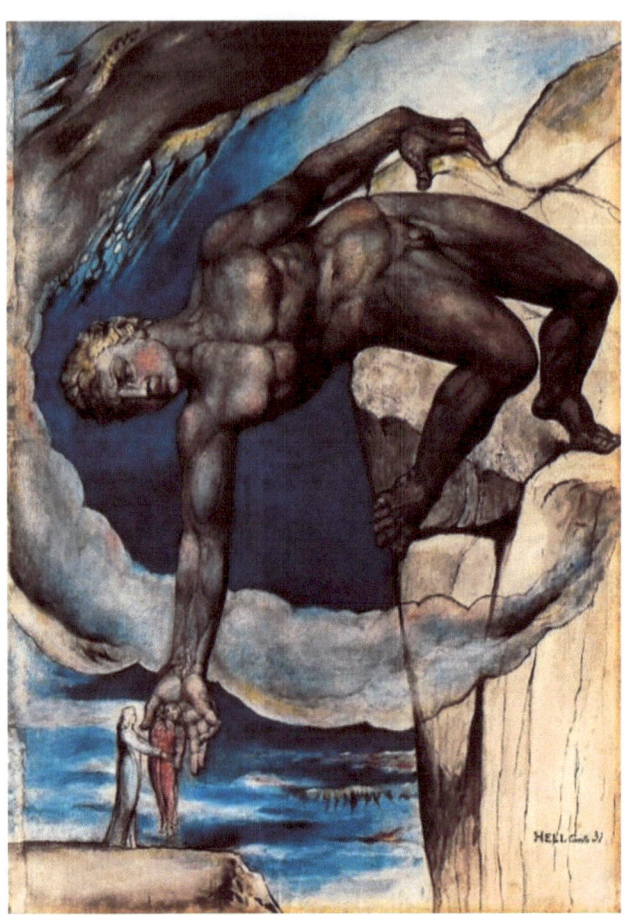

Antaeus setting down Dante and Virgil in the last circle of hell

1824, pen, watercolor

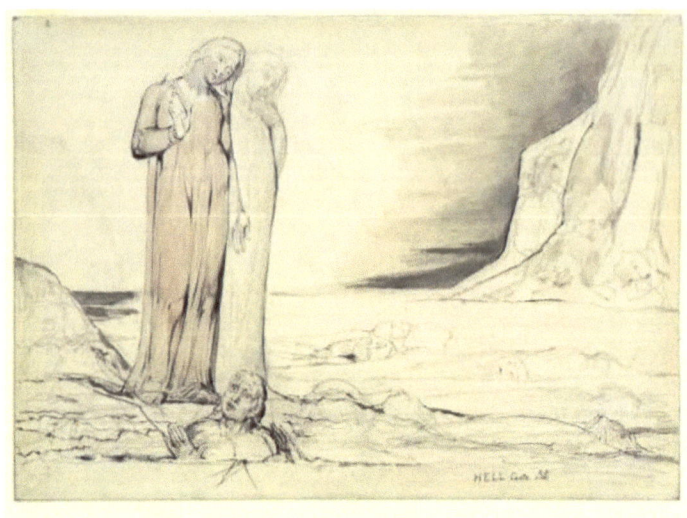

Dante Striking Against Bocca Degli Abbati

1824 - 1827, Pen, pencil, grey wash, and watercolour on paper, 525 x 372 mm, Birmingham Museums & Art Gallery

Between 1824 and 1827 Blake was engaged on a lengthy group of drawings inspired by the work of Dante. Here the scene is that in which Dante stumbles against Boca degli Abati, who had betrayed the Guelphs at the battle of Montaperti (Inferno xxxii, 70-96).

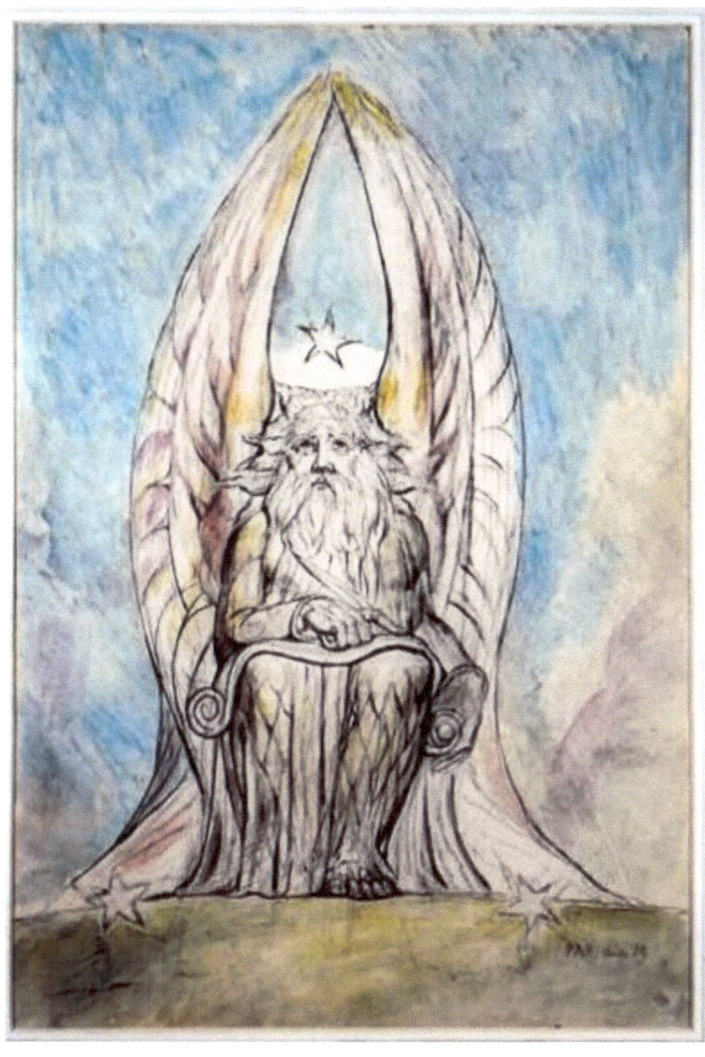

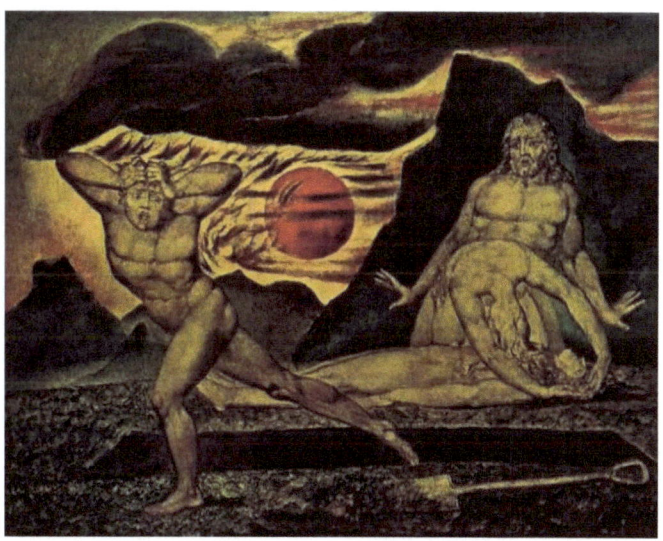

**The Body of Abel Found by Adam & Eve,
c.1825, pen, watercolour and gold**

The Recording Angel

1824 - 1827, Watercolour with pen and ink over
pencil, 520 x 362 mm, Birmingham Museums &
Art Gallery

The scene refers to Dante's 'Divine Comedy:
Paradiso 19' and the Recroding Angel who in the
guise of the 'angel' of convention and tradition
upholds Moral Law. For Blake however,
salvation came through active love and
forgiveness rather than Dante's allusions to the
passive observance of Moral Law.

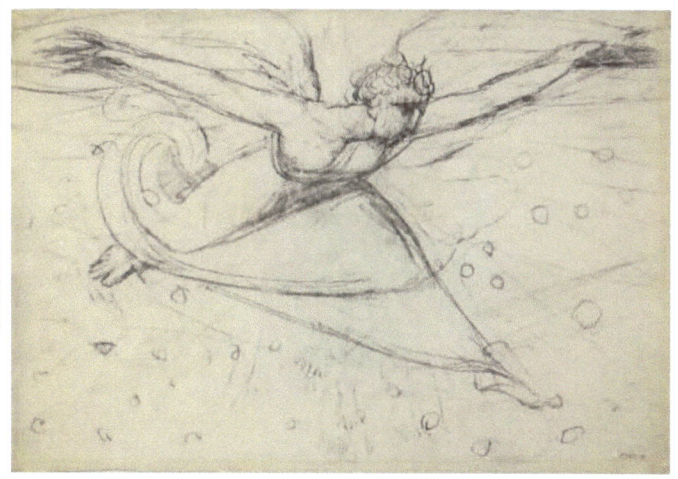

An angel striding among the stars

1827, Pencil drawing, Victoria and Albert
Museum

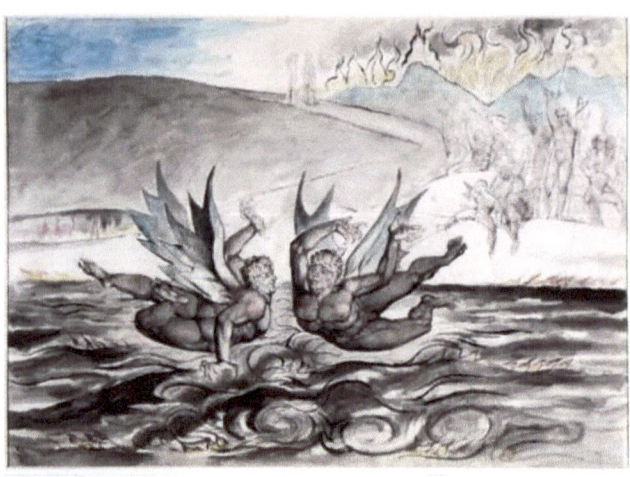

The Baffled Devils Fighting

1824 - 1827, Watercolour with pen and ink over pencil, 369 x 524 mm, Birmingham Museums & Art Gallery

The scene refers to the book 'Divine Comedy, Inferno Canto 22' by Dante, and the battle between two demons, unable to find their victim, who vent their wrath on each other. In their struggle they fall into the boiling pool.

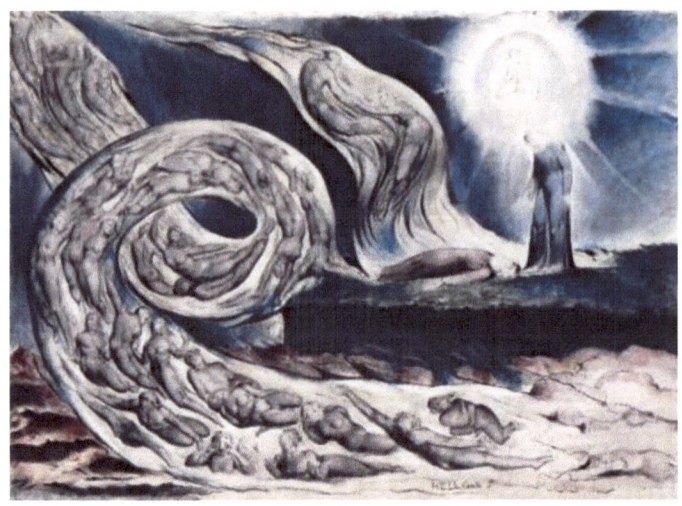

The Circle of the Lustful

1824 - 1827, Pen, ink and watercolour over pencil, with some scratching out, 370 x 523 mm, Birmingham Museums & Art Gallery

This is the most celebrated of William Blake's illustrations to Dante's 'Divine Comedy' commissioned by John Linnell. Blake followed Dante's narrative, but his interpretation of the story is original. This scene illustrates the scene in the Inferno, the journey through Hell, when Dante and Virgil meet the adulturous lovers Francesca da Rimini and Paolo.

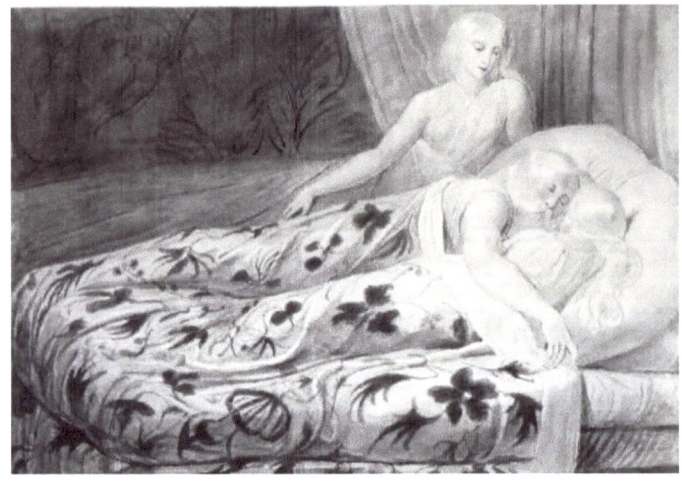

Har and Heva asleep with Mnetha guarding them Illustrations to Tiriel

N.d., pen and grey wash over traces of black chalk on paper, 192 x 280 mm, Fitzwilliam Museum at the University of Cambridge

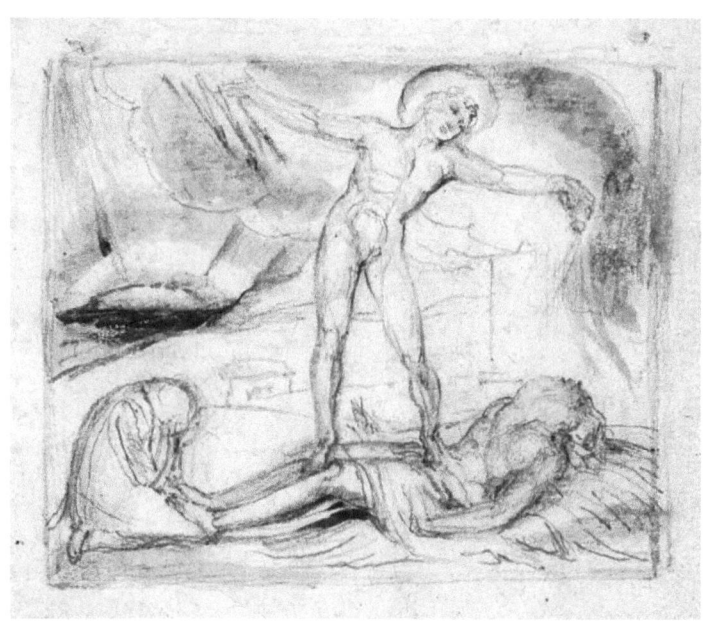

Satan smiting job with boils Illustrations for the Book of Job

N.d., graphite, Indian ink, and grey wash on paper, 97 x 115 mm, Fitzwilliam Museum at the University of Cambridge

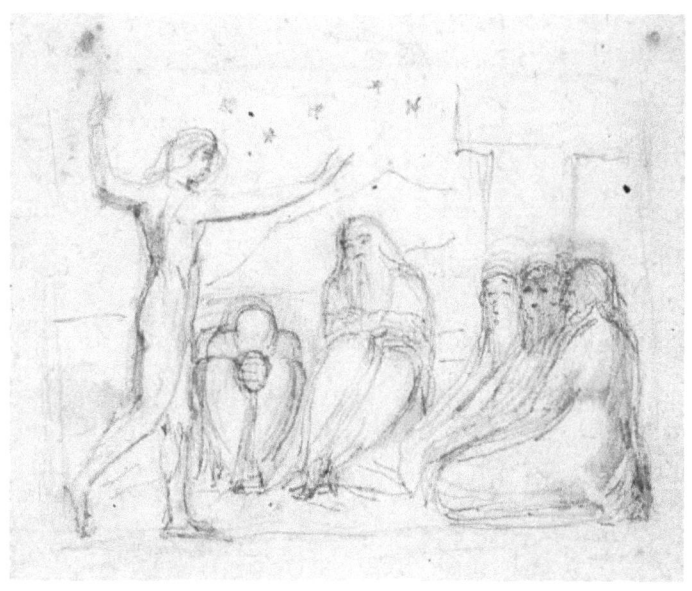

The Wrath of Elihu Illustrations for the Book of Job

N.d., graphite with grey wash on paper, 92 x 124 mm, Fitzwilliam Museum at the University of Cambridge

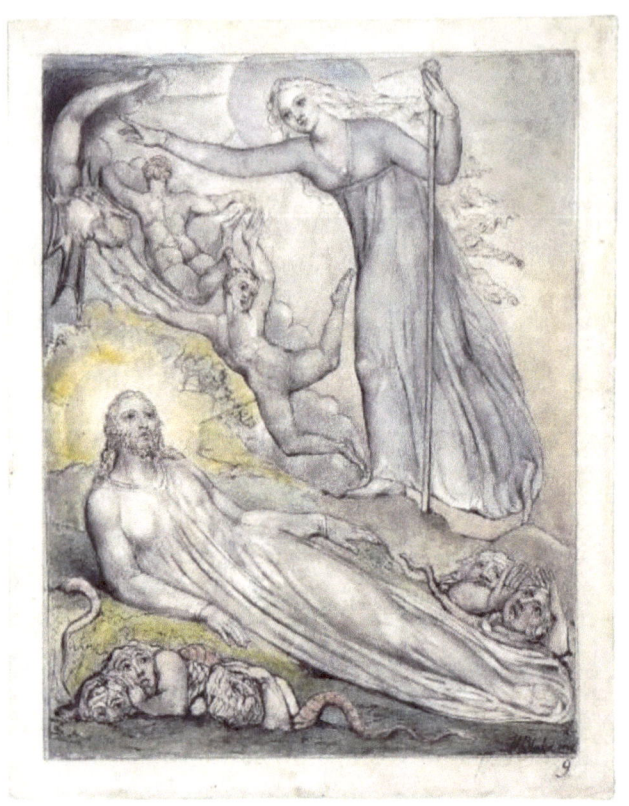

Morning chasing away the phantoms Paradise Regained

N.d., pen, Indian ink, grey wash and watercolour on paper, 165 x 130 mm, Fitzwilliam Museum at the University of Cambridge

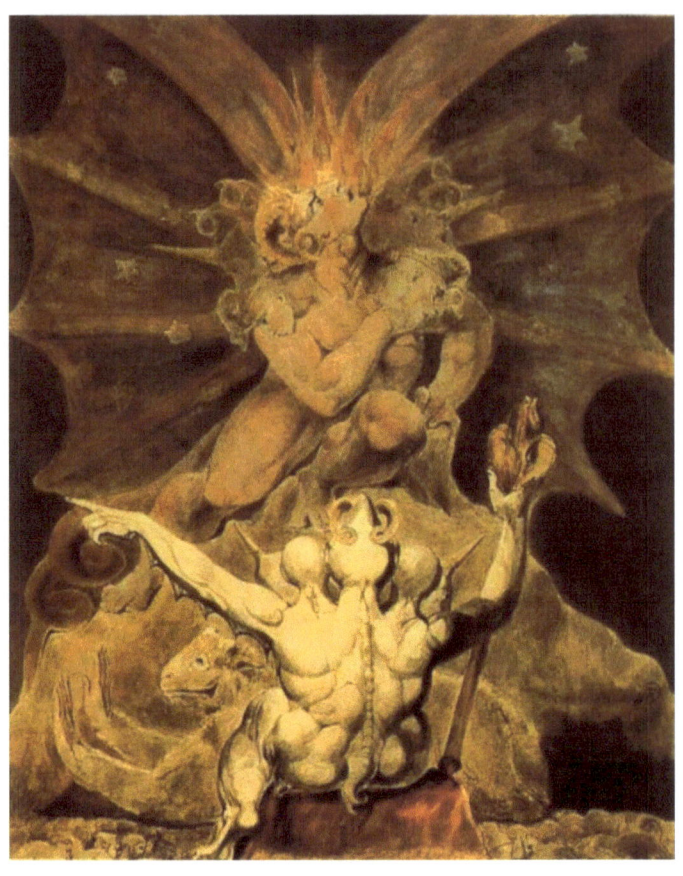

The number of the beast is 666

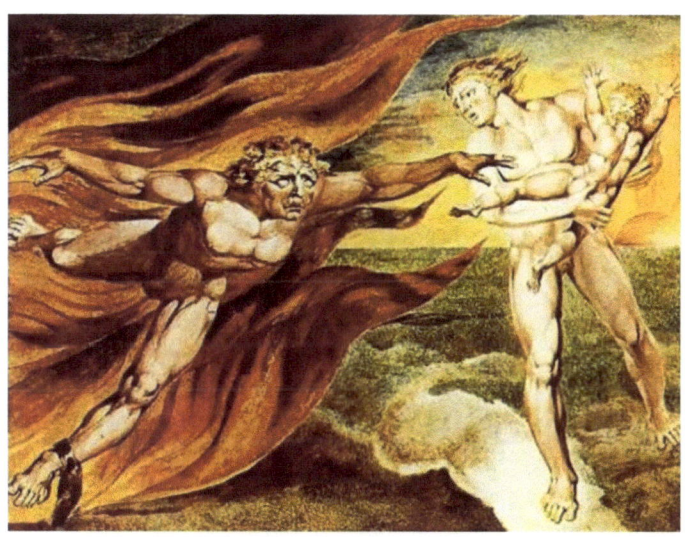

The Good and Evil Angels

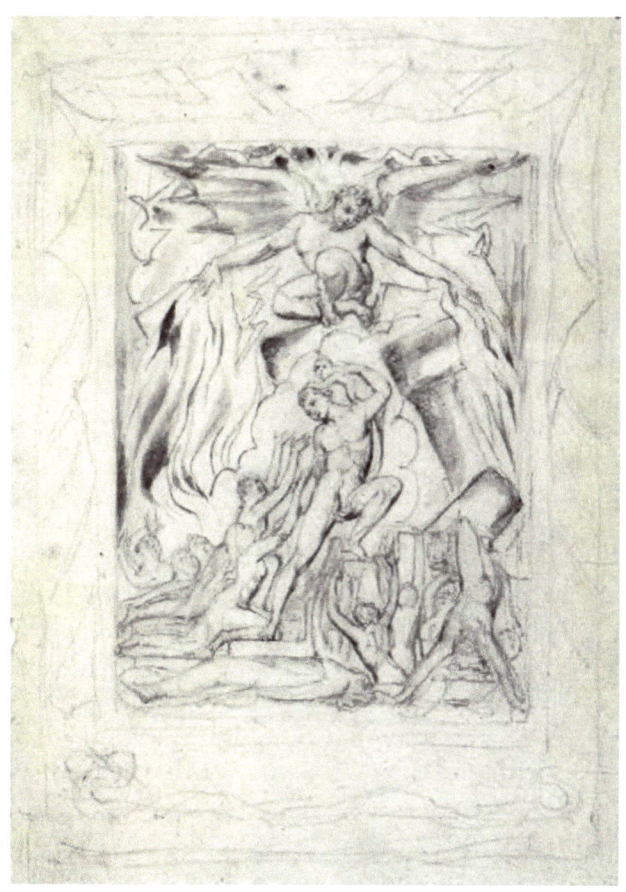

Job's sons and daughters overwhelmed by Satan Illustrations for the Book of Job

N.d., graphite, Indian ink, and grey wash on paper, with slight indications of marginal design in graphite, 127 x 95 mm, Fitzwilliam Museum at the University of Cambridge

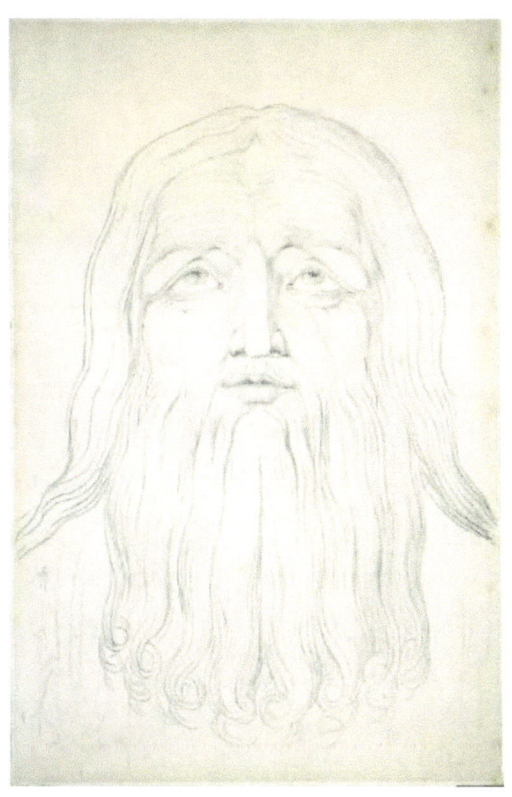

Head of Job

N.d., graphite on paper, 314 x 200 mm, Fitzwilliam Museum at the University of Cambridge

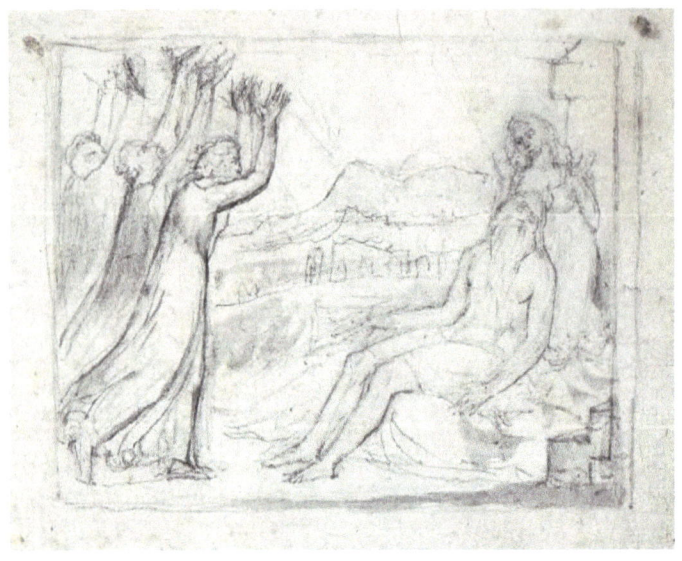

Job's comforters Illustrations for the Book of Job

N.d., pen and graphite, and touches of grey wash on paper, 92 x 114 mm, Fitzwilliam Museum at the University of Cambridge

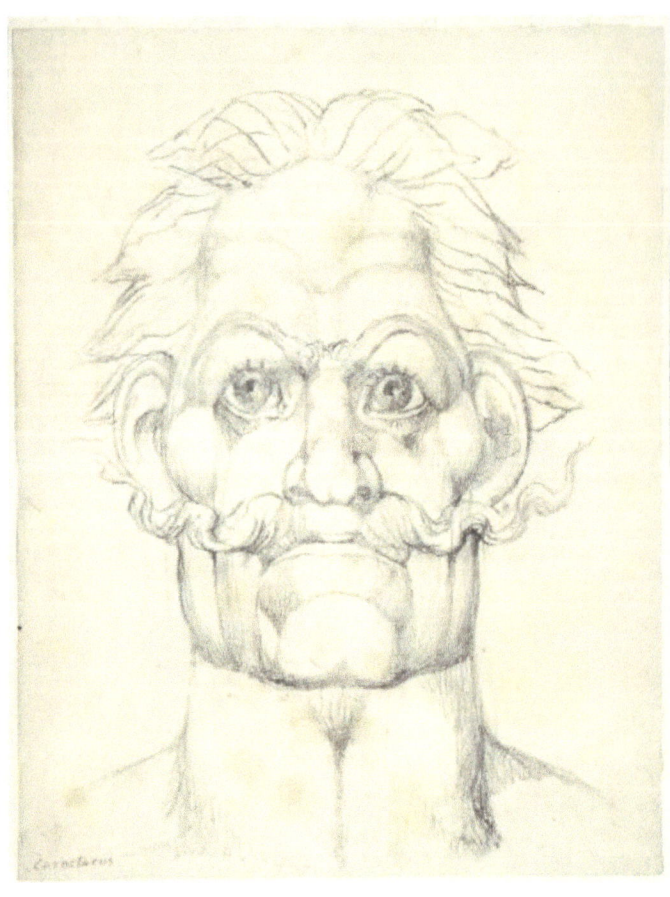

Caractacus

N.d., graphite on paper, 195 x 152 mm, Fitzwilliam Museum at the University of Cambridge

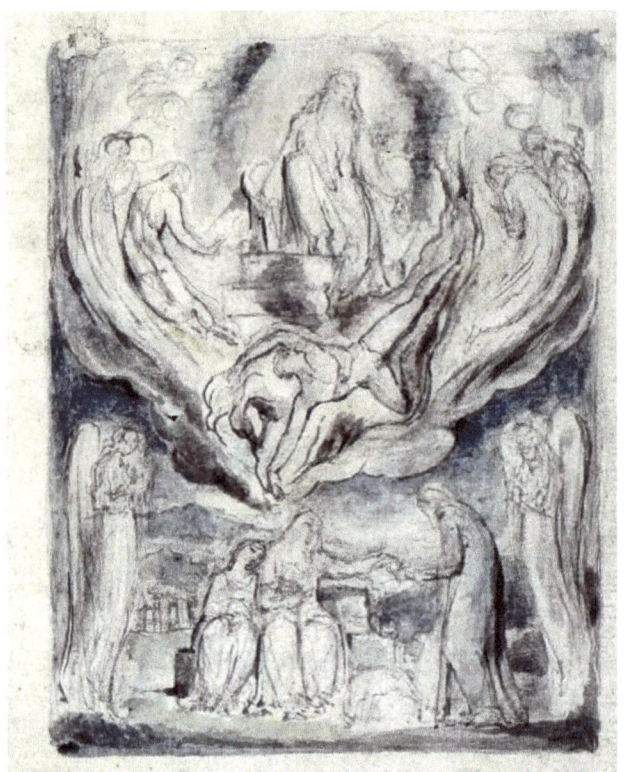

Satan going forth from the presence of God Illustrations for the Book of Job

N.d., graphite, Indian ink, and colour washes on paper, 133 x 112 mm, Fitzwilliam Museum at the University of Cambridge

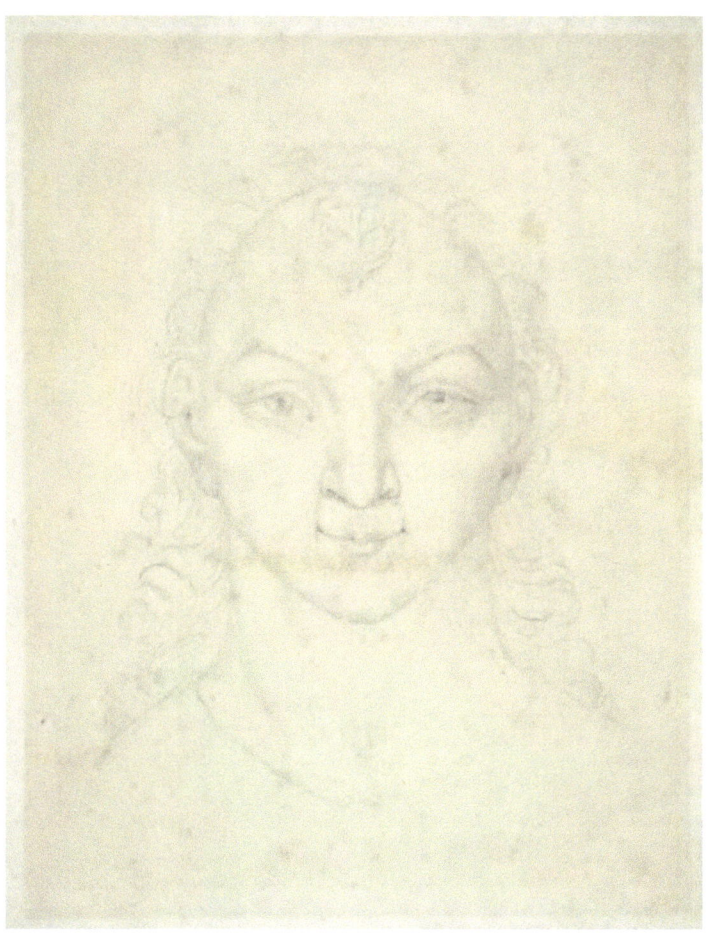

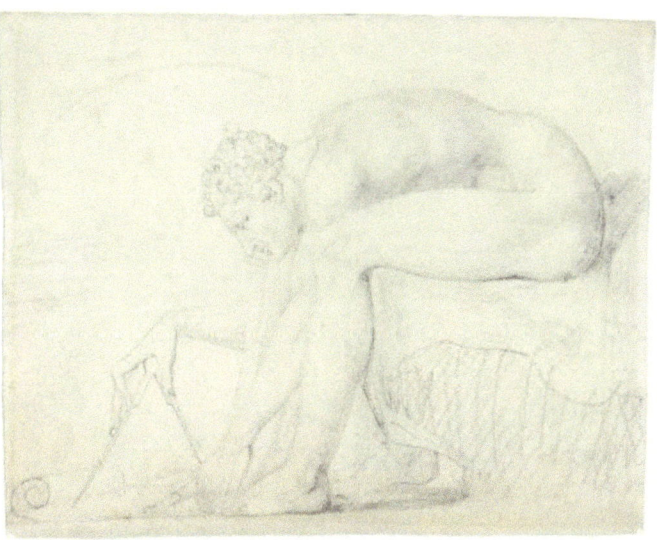

Sir Isaac Newton

N.d., graphite on paper, 355 x 390 mm,
Fitzwilliam Museum at the University of
Cambridge

**The Man who taught Blake painting in his
dreams**

N.d., graphite on paper, 300 x 245 mm,
Fitzwilliam Museum at the University of
Cambridge

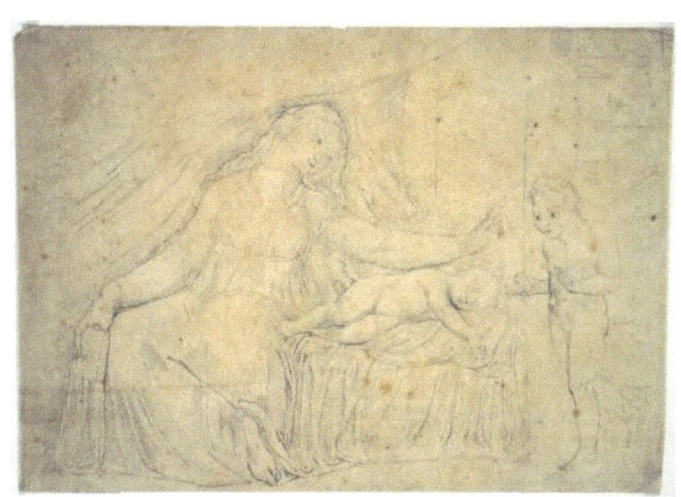

**Tracing of 'The Virgin hushing the young
baptist, who approaches the sleeping infant
Jesus'**

N.d., graphite on paper, 270 x 390 mm,
Fitzwilliam Museum at the University of
Cambridge

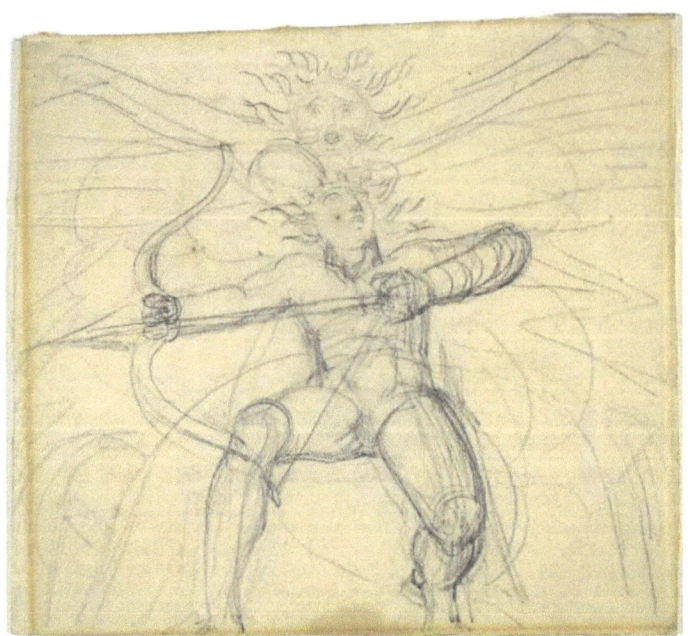

Hyperion ('The Bowman'), Study for Gray's 'Poems'

N.d., graphite on paper, 198 x 192 mm, Fitzwilliam Museum at the University of Cambridge

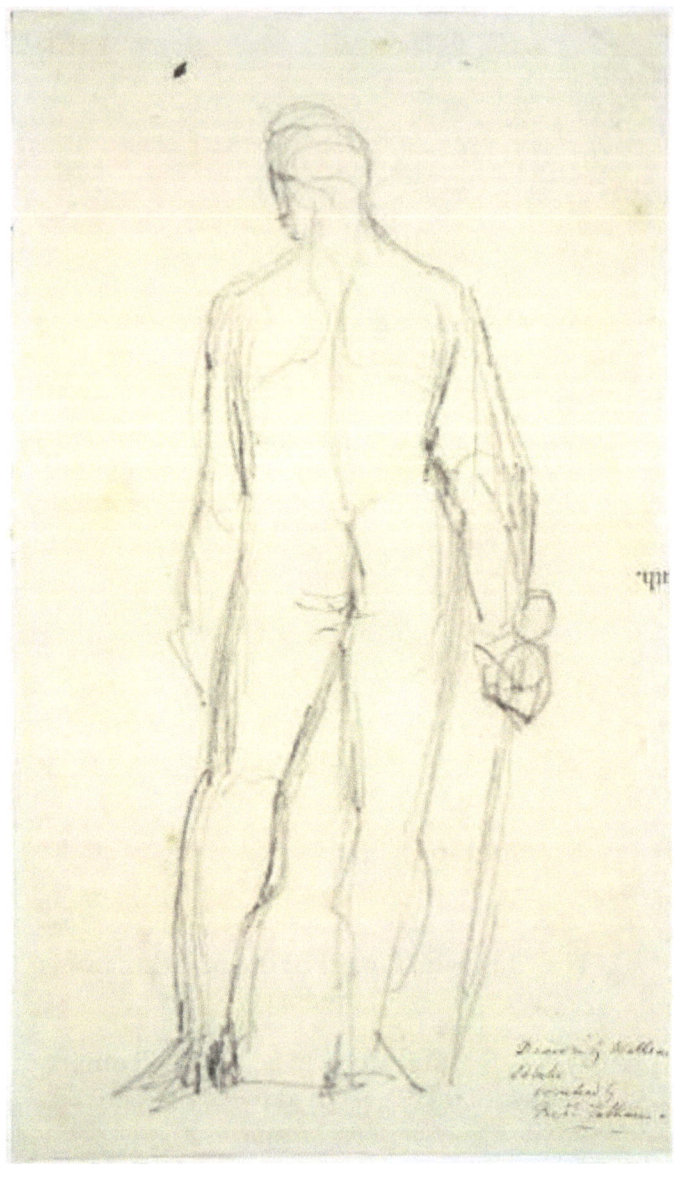

A devil holding a sword, possibly for 'The Schismatics and Sowers of Discord' or for 'Job',

N.d., graphite on paper, 216 x 128 mm, Fitzwilliam Museum at the University of Cambridge

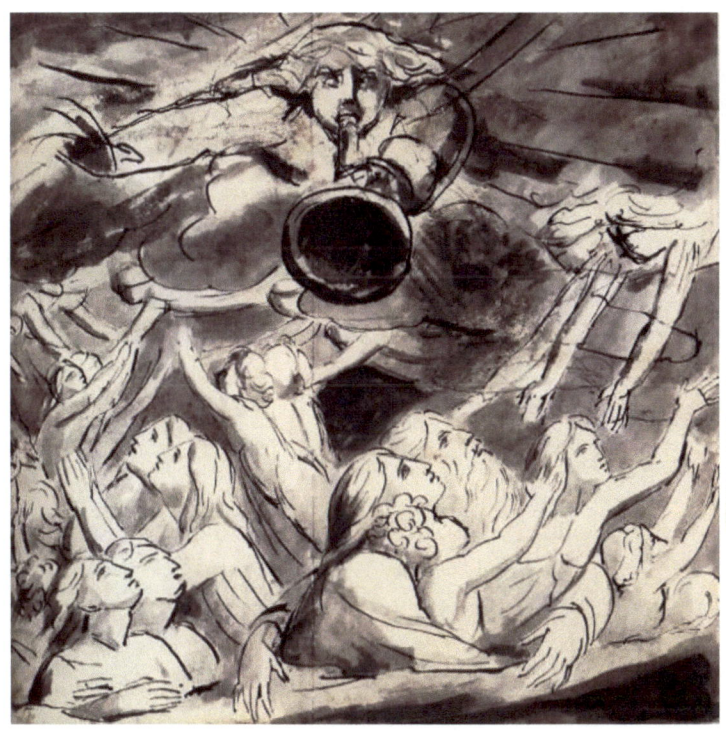

The Resurrection

N.d., Watercolour over pencil on pap, 21 x 20.5
cm, Private collection

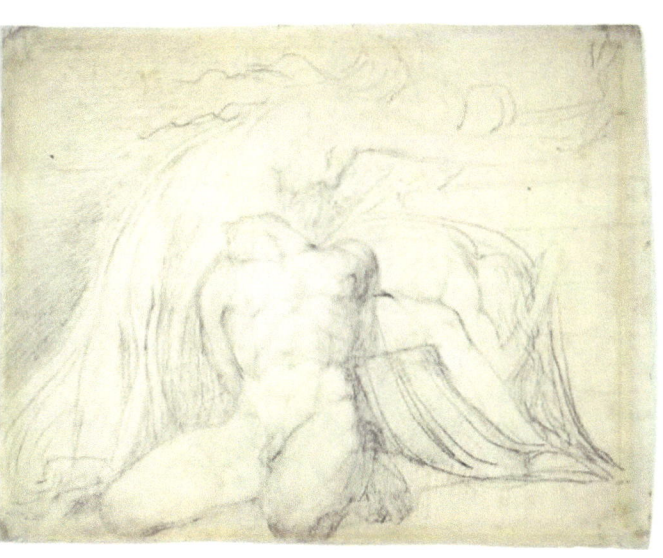

**'The Death Chamber', possible sketch for
Jerusalem', plate 25**

N.d., graphite on paper, 248 x 326 mm,
Fitzwilliam Museum at the University of
Cambridge

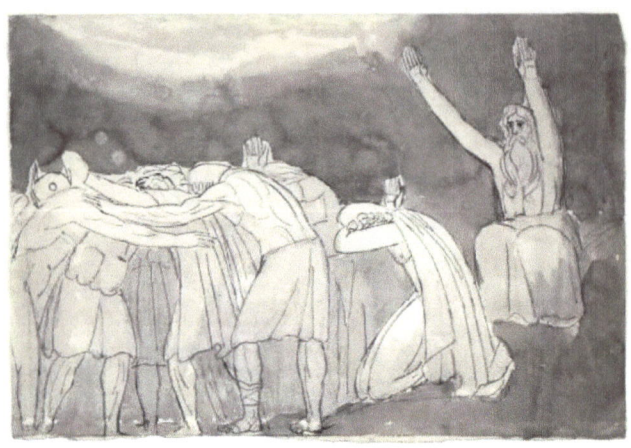

A Druid Ceremony

N.d., pen and grey wash over graphite, 212 x 320 mm, Fitzwilliam Museum at the University of Cambridge

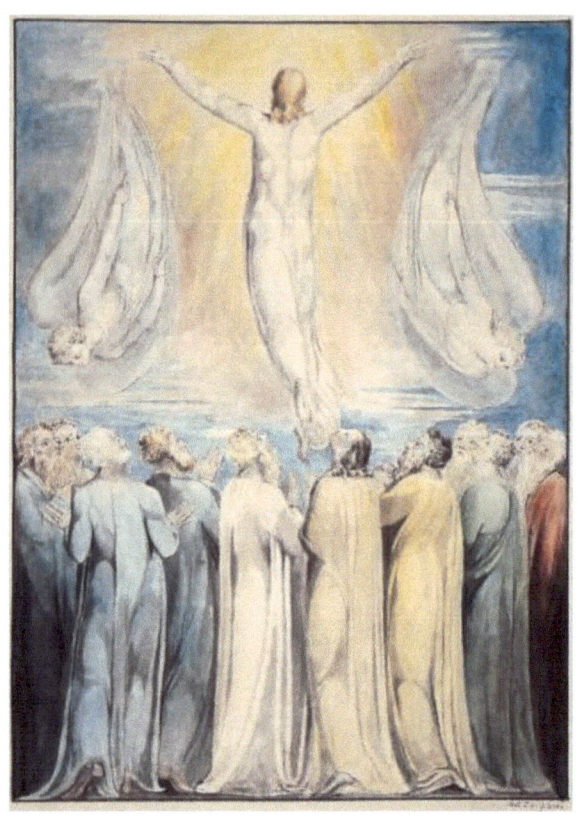

The Ascension

N.d., pen, graphite, Indian ink and watercolour with graphite underdrawing on paper, 425 x 319mm, Fitzwilliam Museum at the University of Cambridge

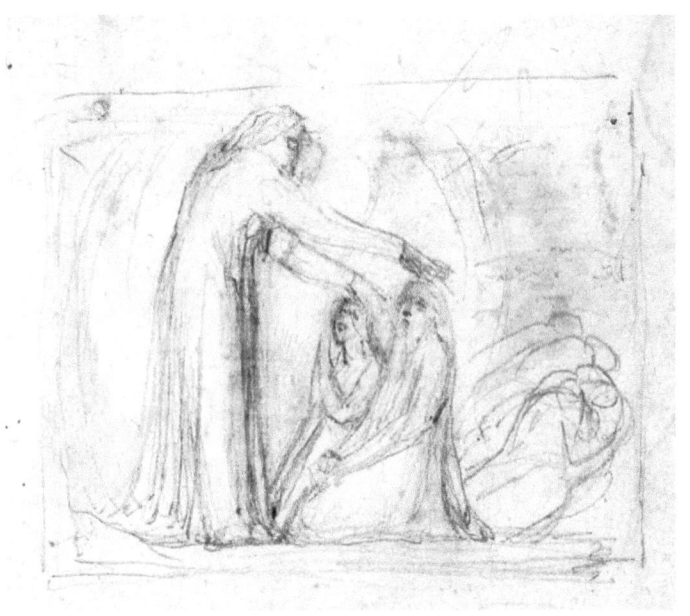

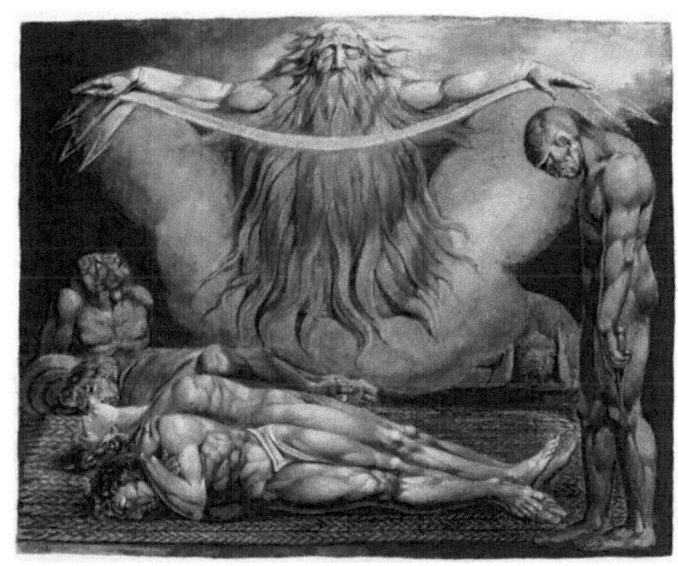

The House of Death

The vision of Christ Illustrations for the Book of Job

N.d., graphite and grey wash on paper, 97 x 117 mm, Fitzwilliam Museum at the University of Cambridge